Hiiii!

...your favorite cosplay YouTuber, Proppen!

Mrowr!

For today's livestream, I'm in Shinjuku at the crack of dawn to try to teach crows how to talk!

I'm dressed up as Killer Whale from The Sharkborg from Hell series!

CAN: APPLY WITH YOUR CHILLED SODA AND WIN.

THIS CHICK'S AS DUMB AS EVER.

DOESN'T SHE REALIZE IT'S THREE IN THE MORNING?

HA HA HA!

Aha! There they are! It's some crow friends!

HUH. THAT'S RIGHT IN OUR NEIGHBORHOOD.

Huh?

For some reason... this street's meowfully cold...

Huh? What is that?

Mrowr? What are mew all looking at?

Wha...?

No way...... What the...?

Wow! Oh wow!

What is that!? What the heck is that!?

?

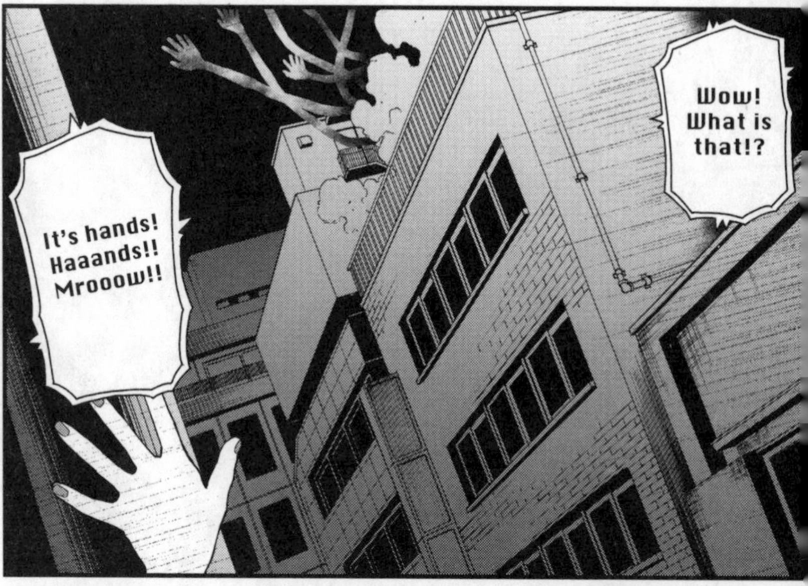
Wow! What is that!?
It's hands! Haaands!! Mrooow!!

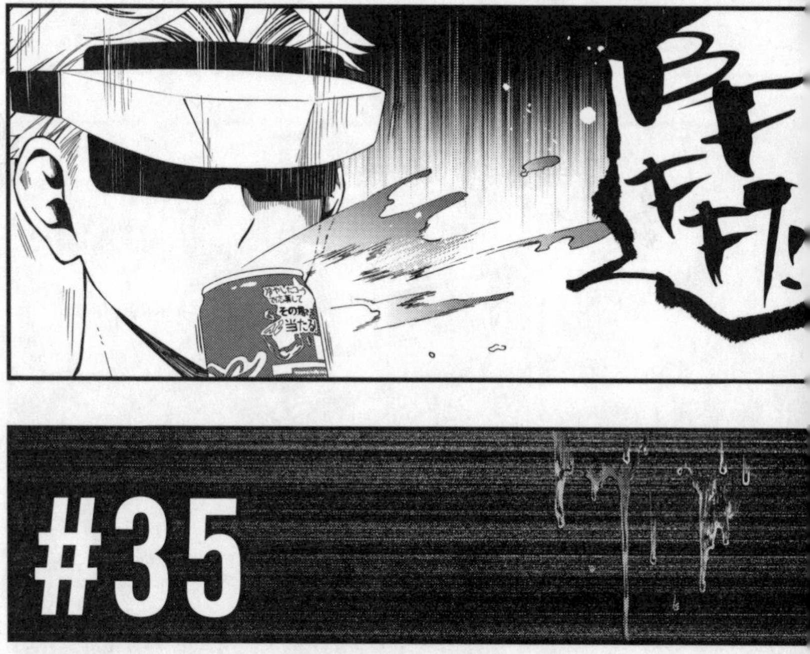

#35

UUUGH, TOOK YOU LONG ENOUGH, IWA-SAN.

YO.

SORRY, SORRY.

I GOT CALLED INTO INVESTIGATION HQ ON MY WAY OVER.

EVEN THOUGH WE KNOW FOR SURE THAT SOLITAIRE WAS THERE.

WITHOUT PERMISSION FROM THE LANDLORD OR A WARRANT, WE CAN'T BLOCKADE THE BUILDING.

AND I THOUGHT I TOLD YOU... TO CATCH AND ARREST HIM...

...HER.

THE OWNER OF THE BUILDING... THAT'D BE...

WELL?

WHO TOLD YOU ABOUT THIS PLACE?

WE HEARD THAT THE YOUTOUKOROU BAR IN SHINJUKU HAS A SPECIAL *HALF-BASEMENT* LEVEL.

HM.

MISTER DAREN.

IT'S AN HONOR...

THE SHINJUKU "MEDIATORS" ARE FAMOUS AMONG HIT MEN.

YOU'RE KNOWN FOR HAVING RELAXED RULES AND A HOMEY ATMOSPHERE.

AH, IF HE INTRODUCED YOU, THEN YOU'RE GOOD.

WELL, WE'D HEARD LOTS OF RUMORS ABOUT THIS PLACE ALREADY.

...RINNE HOROJIMA, HIIRO HOROJIMA...

...I DON'T RECALL GIVING OUT OUR REAL NAMES, EVEN IN SHIBUYA.

...FOR THE HOROJIMA SIBLINGS, KNOWN, AT ONE TIME, AS THE ACES OF SHIBUYA, TO SPEAK SO HIGHLY OF US.

OH, I'M SORRY.

SINCE IT TOOK SO LITTLE TO DIG UP THE INFORMATION, I DIDN'T THINK YOU WERE TRYING TO HIDE IT.

OUR RULES MAY BE RELAXED, BUT......

...WHEN YOU OVERSTEP YOUR BOUNDS, THE CONSEQUENCES CAN BE SCARY.

WHY, THANK YOU.

DON'T TELL ME. YOU'RE A NASTY?

HMM.

GIRI
(SQUEEZE)

HNH...

NGH...

...DIS-RESPECT... CLARISSA......

...DON'T YOU DARE...

ブラん
BURAN
(DANGLE)

ガ
ガシ
GASHI
(GRAB)

ミ

CUTE.

SO CUTE.

ぶん
BUN

ぶん
BUN
(FLAIL)

JUST 'COS YOU'RE HUGE DOESN'T MEAN YOU'RE...

...A BIG DEAL!

I'M SUUUPER-MAD NOW!

CUTE.

CUTE.

AFTER ALL, IT LOOKS LIKE WE'LL BE GETTING PRETTY BUSY.

ANYWAY, I ALWAYS WELCOME NEW PEOPLE TO TAKE ON WORK FOR ME.

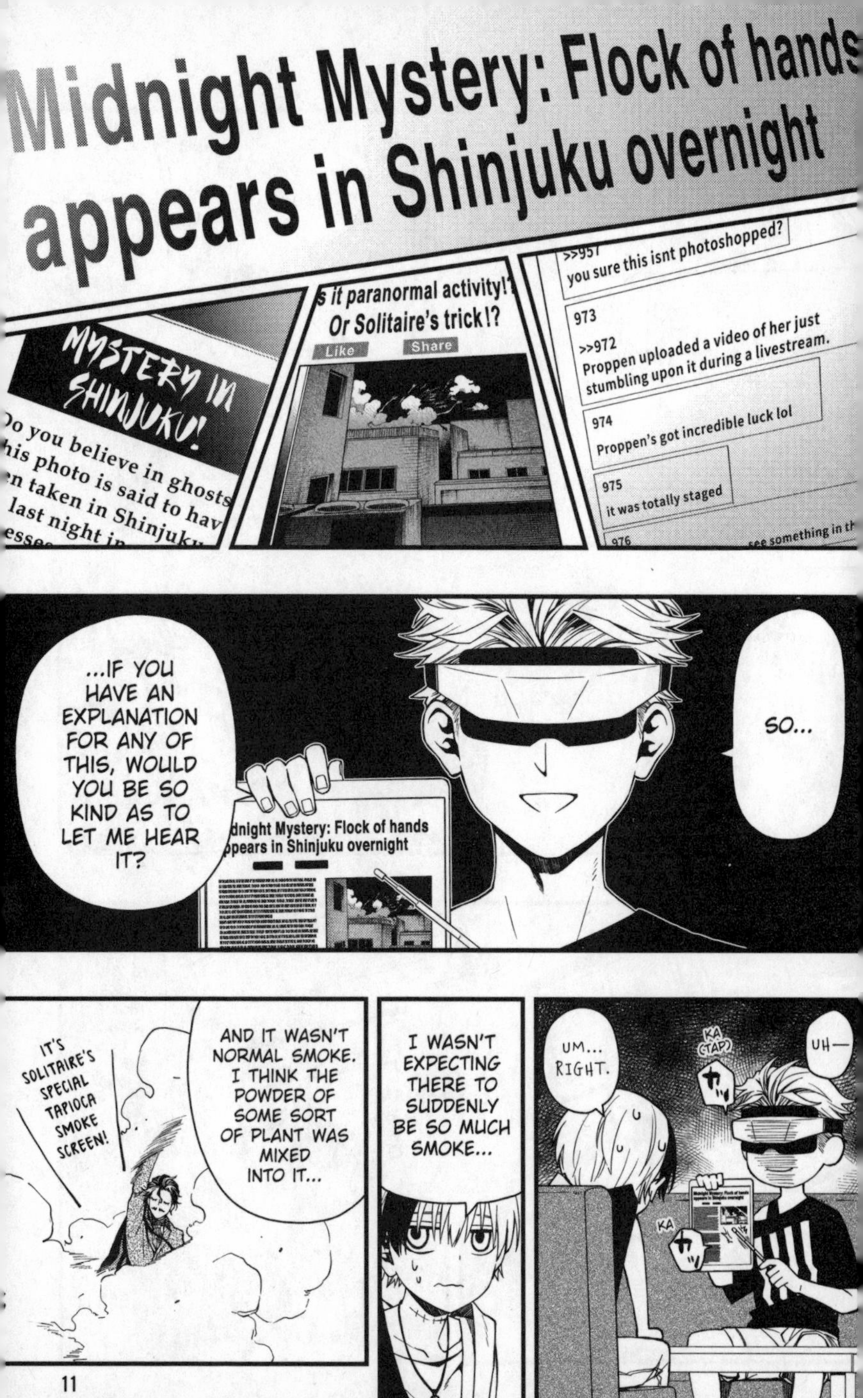

Midnight Mystery: Flock of hands appears in Shinjuku overnight
>>957
you sure this isnt photoshopped?
973
>>972
Proppen uploaded a video of her just stumbling upon it during a livestream.
974
Proppen's got incredible luck lol
975
it was totally staged
s it paranormal activity!?
Or Solitaire's trick!?
Like
Share
MYSTERY IN SHINJUKU!
SO...
...IF YOU HAVE AN EXPLANATION FOR ANY OF THIS, WOULD YOU BE SO KIND AS TO LET ME HEAR IT?
dnight Mystery: Flock of hands
ppears in Shinjuku overnight
UH—
KA (TAP)
KA
UM... RIGHT.
I WASN'T EXPECTING THERE TO SUDDENLY BE SO MUCH SMOKE...
AND IT WASN'T NORMAL SMOKE. I THINK THE POWDER OF SOME SORT OF PLANT WAS MIXED INTO IT...
IT'S SOLITAIRE'S SPECIAL TAPIOCA SMOKE SCREEN!

...I THINK WE'LL HAVE TO USE THE BACK ENTRANCE FOR A LITTLE WHILE.

GASHI (SKRITCH)
がじ

GASHI
がじ

HAAAH.

LOOK, IF YOU WANT TO PUT YOUR PLANS FOR A PEACEFUL LIFE ON THE BACK BURNER, THAT'S UP TO YOU...

ザワ
ZAWA

ザワ
ZAWA (MURMUR)

PASHA (SNAP)
ぱしゃ

SOLITAIRE WAS HERE!

THIS IS THE PLACE. RIGHT HERE.

APRON: HIMAWARI USED BOOKSTORE

......I'M SORRY.

I'M NOT INTERESTED IN BEING THE CENTER OF THAT MUCH ATTENTION, OKAY?

I USED SPIRIT-OF-THE-DEAD THREAD TO GIVE THE INVISIBLE HANDS OF THE SPIRITS THE ABILITY TO INTERACT WITH PHYSICAL THINGS......

IN A SENSE.

WERE YOU CONTROLLING ALL THESE HANDS?

SOLITAIRE, OBVIOUSLY, AND LEMMINGS MIGHT HAVE REALIZED IT TOO.

GOOD QUESTION...

WELL, THE PUBLIC IS SPLIT BETWEEN THOSE WHO THINK IT WAS ONE OF SOLITAIRE'S TRICKS AND THOSE WHO SUSPECT PARANORMAL ACTIVITY......

BUT HOW MANY PEOPLE KNOW FOR SURE IT WASN'T JUST A MAGIC TRICK?

...EVEN THOUGH I HID AFTER IT WAS DONE, HE SUDDENLY DISAPPEARED, SO I'M NOT SURE......

ALSO...... XIAOYU WAS ON THE ROOF AT THE TIME, BUT...

Master

TA (TAP)

UUUH... WELL, FOR NOW, HOW ABOUT ARASE AND I GO IN AGAIN?

SO WHAT DO WE DO, BOSS?

...GEH.

......A REAL PAIN-IN-THE-ASS JOURNALIST IS HERE.

......I THINK WE'D BETTER FORGET THAT IDEA, IWA-SAN.

WHAT IS IT?

HIS FACE LOOKED COMPLETELY DIFFERENT, BUT THE COLOR OF HIS SOUL WAS IDENTICAL.

...CONSIDERING WHAT'S BEEN ON THE NEWS TOO, YOU THINK THAT GUY WHO CAME IN FOR A READING WAS SOLITAIRE?

OKAY, SO...

YOU WOULDN'T HAPPEN TO REMEMBER A GIRL IN A WHEELCHAIR... WHO HAD A LONG BRAID HANGING HALFWAY DOWN HER BACK... WOULD YOU?

AS WAS THE SOUL HAUNTING HIM.

WELL...

AND WHAT ABOUT THE HIGH SCHOOL GIRL?

I SEE.

AROO?

NEVER DISAPPEAR ON ME AGAIN, YOU HEAR?

AWWW, TOYOMARU!

むに (MOOSH)
MUNI

むに
MUNI

THE GIRL SIMPLY WON'T SHOW HER TRUE COLORS.

IT'S NO USE, CORPSE GOD-SAMA.

THERE, THERE, THERE!

AND HER DOG'S TAIL IS MOST ADORABLE!

WHAT'S THAT ALL ABOUT...?

WELL... APPARENTLY, THE DOG WAS AT HOME THE WHOLE TIME.

HUH? SO THERE REALLY WAS A DOG?

BUT FOR SOME REASON, SHE REALLY SEEMS TO BELIEVE THAT HER PET RAN AWAY FROM HOME.

17

HUH?

AND THE MAN WHO CLAIMED TO BE HER FATHER SPLIT FROM HER ALONG THE WAY.

ACKET: WATCH OUT FOR FIRES

......
......

COULD HE HAVE BEEN HER SUGAR DADDY...?

...

HER REAL FATHER IS SOMEONE ELSE ENTIRELY AND WAS AT HOME AS WELL.

SORRY. MY BAD.

SUGAR PATTY!

SUGAR PATTY?

?

18

THAT HE CAME ASKING QUESTIONS ABOUT THAT SYMBOL TELLS ME HE TARGETED US FROM THE VERY START.

STILL... WHAT DREW SOLITAIRE'S ATTENTION TO US?

NOW FOR THE MAIN ISSUE—

GUESS I'D BETTER REPORT THIS TO CLARISSA TOO.

...

THAT... WRITING ON THE WALL—FROM THE LOOKS OF IT, IT COULD BE FIRE-BREATHING BUG......

WHAT DID THEY MEAN BY "BASTARD CHILD OF SABARAMOND"?

DOES "SABARAMOND" MEAN SOMETHING IN THE WORLD YOU'RE FROM?

IT WAS ENOUGH TO MAKE YOU FLY OFF THE HANDLE AND CAST THAT HUGE SPELL.

...I HAVE NO IDEA.

...

LORD ARIUS SABARA-MOND...

THE COUNTRY MY MASTER AND I LIVED IN OVER ONE HUNDRED YEARS AGO.

...WAS THE HEAD COURT SORCERER OF THE BYANDY EMPIRE—

SIGN: SHIBUYA STATION

UNDER-
STOOD.

WE'LL TAKE
THE SAME
PRECAUTIONS
WE DID FIVE
YEARS AGO...
WHEN IT WAS
HOSOROGI.

YES.

UH-
HUH.

ALL
UNDER THE
PROTECTION
OF SABARA-
MOND.

21

THOSE SNIPERS HAVE SKIPPED TOWN, THOUGH—

THAT'S FINE.

THERE'S ONLY AN OPENING FOR ONE WITHIN THE AGAKURA.

#36

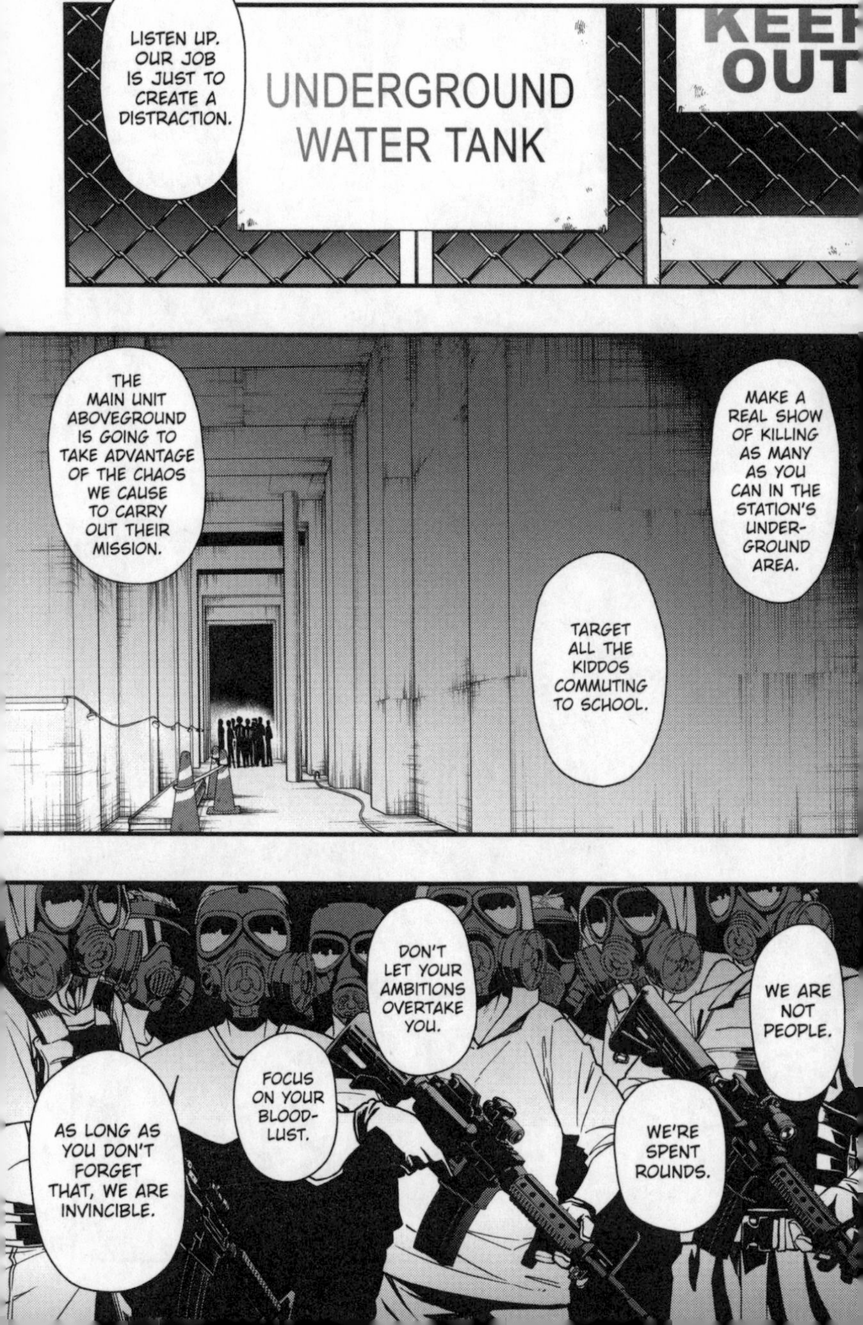
UNDERGROUND WATER TANK
LISTEN UP. OUR JOB IS JUST TO CREATE A DISTRACTION.
THE MAIN UNIT ABOVEGROUND IS GOING TO TAKE ADVANTAGE OF THE CHAOS WE CAUSE TO CARRY OUT THEIR MISSION.
MAKE A REAL SHOW OF KILLING AS MANY AS YOU CAN IN THE STATION'S UNDER-GROUND AREA.
TARGET ALL THE KIDDOS COMMUTING TO SCHOOL.
WE ARE NOT PEOPLE.
WE'RE SPENT ROUNDS.
DON'T LET YOUR AMBITIONS OVERTAKE YOU.
FOCUS ON YOUR BLOOD-LUST.
AS LONG AS YOU DON'T FORGET THAT, WE ARE INVINCIBLE.

AND TODAY, WE'RE GOING TO PROVE THAT...

WE ARE NOT INFERIOR TO THE HEILEI CLAN, AGAKURA'S BOYS, OR EVEN THE FOLLOWERS OF CRAZY BONES KAGURA!

WHAT THE......?

24

WHEN DID HE GET HERE!?

AND WHAT THE HELL—?

IN THE BACK THERE...

!?

NOTH-ING...

WHAT'S THE MATTER?

HOW'S HE SO TALL!?

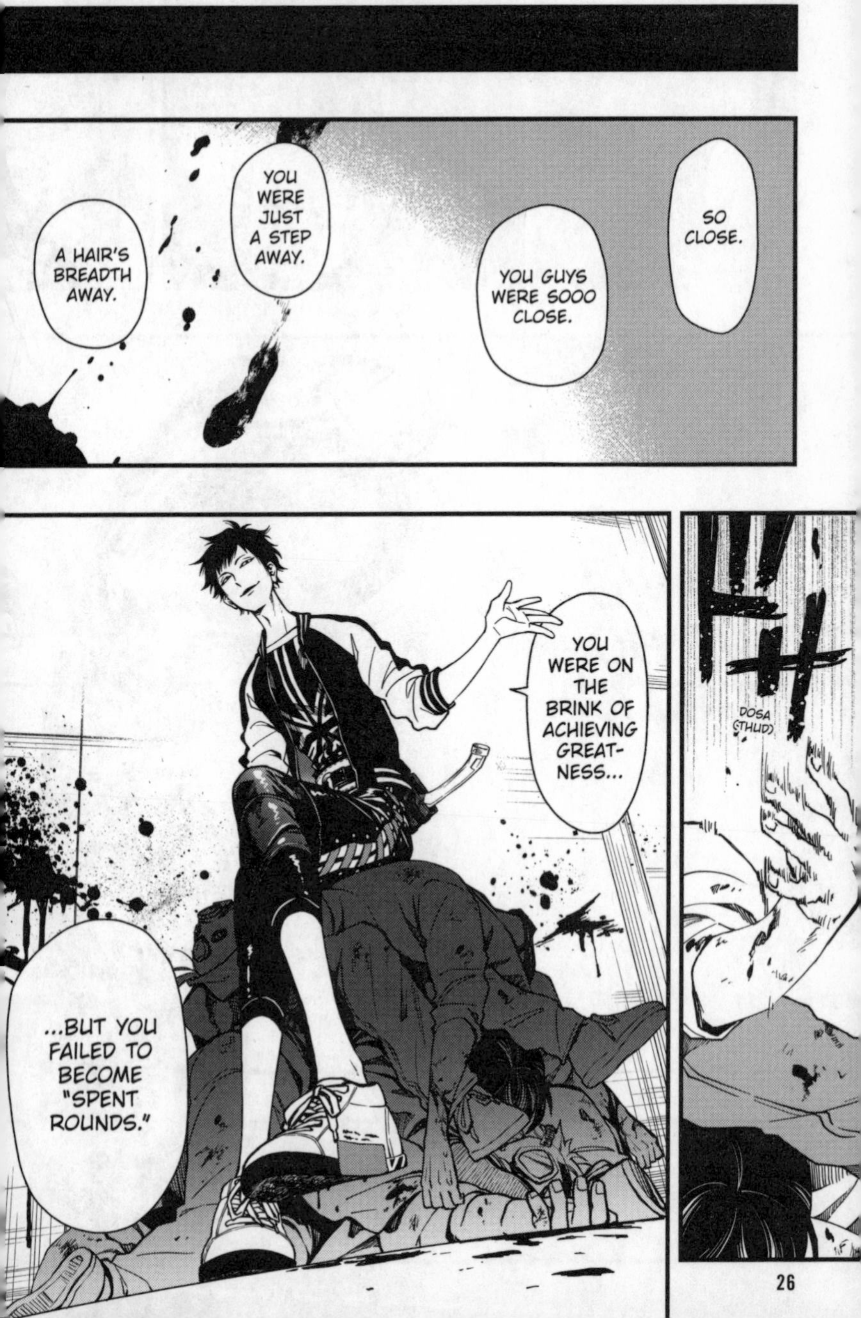
SO CLOSE.
YOU GUYS WERE SOOO CLOSE.
YOU WERE JUST A STEP AWAY.
A HAIR'S BREADTH AWAY.
DOSA (THUD)
YOU WERE ON THE BRINK OF ACHIEVING GREATNESS...
...BUT YOU FAILED TO BECOME "SPENT ROUNDS."

BULLETS MUSTN'T BE SO SCARED.

TSK, TSK.

HYOI (LIFT)

REDUCED TO DISGUSTING, BLOODRED HUNKS OF MEAT.

BLAM, BLAM, BLAM, BLAM! I'D BE DEAD.

WITH YOUR GUNS.

...YOU'D HAVE GOTTEN ME WAY BEFORE I GOT YOU.

IF NOT FOR THAT...

...PROVED YOU WEREN'T INFERIOR TO AGAKURA.

DOCHA (SPLAT)

AT LEAST YOU GUYS...

...REMARK-ABLY...

I DIDN'T REALLY KNOW MUCH ABOUT THEM. COULD IT BE THEY WERE ACTUALLY WICKED-STRONG?

MAYBE EVEN THE STRONGEST IN THE WORLD?

...ALL DONE.

IT WAS A CLOSE ONE. I COULD'VE DIED.

ZAAAA (CRACKLE)

Momo-ya?

How are things there?

No casualties. It was over in five seconds.

THAT'S A SHAME.

HOW MANY DEAD?

HOW ARE THE GIRLS? THEY WERE HANDLING THESE GUYS' MAIN UNIT, RIGHT?

ZAZA

Sorry, but while I've got you, you've got a new gig, Momoya.

HMMM.

Appar-ently, the gig's in Shinjuku.

So you've been ordered to pay a visit to the Mediators in Shibuya.

You're off after today, right?

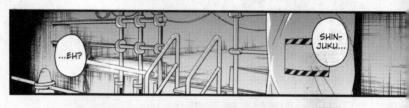

...EH?

SHIN-JUKU...

IF I GET TO MEET THAT SOLITAIRE GUY...

...I HOPE I CAN GET HIS AUTO-GRAPH.

A WORD FOR YOU FIRST, THOUGH.

NOW, BOY...

...STARTING TODAY, YOU WILL BECOME A NECROMANCER.

IT'S NOT REALLY A TALENT.

IN FACT, EVEN YOUR EVIL EYE IS MORE LIKE A "SPIRITUAL DISPOSITION."

GAAAN

...YOU HAVE NO MAGICAL TALENTS.

APART FROM YOUR EVIL EYE'S ABILITY TO SEE SPIRITS...

GAAAN (SHOCK)

...

WHY NOT THE FIRST-RANKED, YOU ASK?

I'M SURPRISED AT YOUR AMBITION TO RISE IN THE WORLD, BOY.

BUT DON'T WORRY.

I'LL STILL TRAIN YOU.

I WILL RAISE YOU TO BE THE TENTH-RANKED COURT SORCERER.

SHUN (SLUMP)

AND I'M IN SECOND PLACE.

BECAUSE UTSUROJUZA, WHO OCCUPIES THE THIRD RANK, IS IN A LEAGUE APART FROM THOSE RANKED FOURTH AND BELOW.

GO (CLACK)

!

THAT'S NOT TRUE.

ABILITY ALONE WON'T CUT IT.

AND THE ONE WHO OCCUPIES FIRST PLACE IS HALF-POLITICIAN.

GO

GO

...YOU SHOULD BE STANDING IN MY POSITION.

IN TERMS OF ABILITY...

YOU'RE BEING APPRAISED ALREADY...

LOOK, BOY.

SO CYNICAL, IZLIZ-SAN.

...YOU WILL BECOME AN INSTRUMENT OF COURT POLITICS IN THE FUTURE.

...TO SEE WHETHER OR NOT...

A PRICE CANNOT BE PUT ON THEM.

ALL PEOPLE ARE EQUALLY VALUABLE.

... RENOWNED THROUGH-OUT THE EMPIRE...

CROWDS OF PEOPLE WOULD FLOCK TO ANY EVENT WHERE LORD SABARAMOND MADE AN APPEARANCE.

LORD SABARAMOND WAS A KIND PERSON...

KANNAGI ...WHO?

SO LIKE WHAT WE'D CALL A CELEBRITY HERE.

LIKE RYOUMA KANNAGI?

I'M SURPRISED YOU KNOW THE NAMES OF ORDINARY IDOLS.

BUT OF COURSE.

AND WOULD YOU STOP BRINGING EVERYTHING BACK TO SHARKS?

I WILL NOT.

...OKAY, THEN.

THE SHARKBORG FROM HELL
THE SHARK SIX

Starring: Sharkborg
Costarring: Ryouma Kannagi,
Mana Kikimura, Rudy Wong

WHEN RYOUMA KANNAGI WAS A CHILD, HE PLAYED A BACKGROUND CHARACTER IN *THE SHARKBORG FROM HELL Z*, AND HE'LL BE REPRISING THE ROLE AS HIS GROWN-UP SELF IN THE LATEST INSTALLMENT SET TO FILM SOON.

THEY'RE MAKING... ANOTHER SEQUEL?

IS THIS WHAT SABARAMOND IS LIKE?

FINE. WE'LL USE RYOUMA KANNAGI AS AN EXAMPLE.

AH, YES. JUST LIKE THAT.

WITHOUT THE DANCING, THOUGH.

EEEK!

WHOO!

JUDGING BY THE BUG'S TONE OF VOICE WHEN THEY SAID, "BASTARD CHILDREN OF SABARAMOND," I SENSED THEIR HOSTILITY AGAINST THE GROUP.

SO HOW DID FIRE-BREATHING BUG KNOW SABARAMOND'S NAME?

THAT'S WHAT'S TROUBLING ME TOO.

I DON'T KNOW WHAT BECAME OF LORD SABARAMOND AFTER THE COLLAPSE OF THE EMPIRE, BUT...

...I BELIEVE A SORCERER OF LORD SABARAMOND'S CALIBER COULD EASILY EXTEND THEIR LIFE BY ONE OR TWO HUNDRED YEARS.

SABARAMOND LIVED A HUNDRED YEARS AGO, RIGHT?

SO AREN'T THEY DEAD BY NOW?

...BUT A CAPABLE ENOUGH SORCERER CAN AT LEAST SLOW DOWN THE AGING PROCESS.

THEY MAY NOT BE LIKE NECROMANCERS, WHO CAN CONTINUE MOVING AFTER HALTING ALL LIFE PROCESSES...

...NOR WOOD MAGES WHO FUSE WITH THE TREES...

WHOA... MAGIC FROM PARALLEL UNIVERSES IS REALLY SOMETHING...

THAT'S NOT WHAT'S IMPORTANT HERE, THOUGH, IS IT?

THAT'S...

...I JUST DON'T WANT TO DREDGE UP OLD MEMORIES.

BUT WHAT IF...

...DOESN'T THAT MEAN YOU HAVE AN ALLY?

IF A COURT SORCERER FROM THAT EMPIRE REALLY IS BEING IMPLICATED IN THIS...

...THIS ORGANIZATION... "THE BASTARD CHILDREN OF SABARAMOND"...

...IS CONNECTED TO THE EMPIRE...?

...THAT I FLED THAT WORLD TO COME TO THIS ONE.

IT WAS SOLELY FOR MY OWN BENEFIT...

EVEN SO...

I'M THE ONE WHO'S NOTHING BUT AN OUTSIDER...

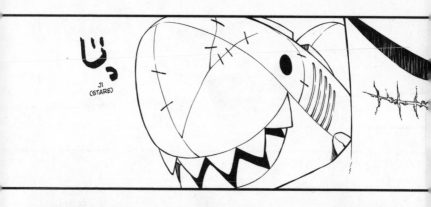

JI
(STARE)

CALM DOWN, XIAOYU.

WHOA, WHOA.

MASTER. WHAT ON EARTH WAS THAT!?

I THOUGHT IT MUST BE SOME KIND OF STEALTH-SUIT TECHNOLOGY I AM UNFAMILIAR WITH, BUT...

SOMETHING INVISIBLE WAS OBSTRUCTING LEMMINGS AND THE OTHER MAN.

...that was no mere sleight of hand.

NOW, LISTEN.

I knew we should be getting rid of him!

Maybe the fake Polka...

There was definitely "something" there. I know it...!!

...DO YOU KNOW SOMETHING I DON'T?

THAT "SOMETHING" DIDN'T ATTACK YOU, RIGHT?

XIAOYU.

WHAT'S THE JOB I ASKED OF YOU?

SO THAT MAKES IT YOUR ALLY.

Good to hear you haven't forgotten.

I—I AM TERRIBLY SORRY, SIR.

.............AND THE FAKE POLKA...

...SIR.

......TO PROTECT MISS SAYO...

STOP THAT. IT DOESN'T SUIT YOU.

...YOU ONLY EVER SPEAK POLITELY TO ME WHEN YOU'RE REALLY DOWN.

BUT AS YOU ARE NOW, YOU WOULDN'T BELIEVE ANYTHING I'D TELL YOU. YOU WOULDN'T BE ABLE TO ACCEPT IT, WOULD YOU?

IT'S TRUE, I KNOW THE FAKE POLKA'S SECRET.

LOOK, EITHER WAY, IT'S NOT SOMETHING I CAN EXPLAIN THROUGH WORDS ALONE.

..........! TH-THAT WAS BECAUSE...

You didn't believe me even when I told you Fake Polka was fine.

TH-THAT'S NOT TRUE...!

IF HE REFUSES TO TELL YOU, I'LL TRY PLEADING WITH HIM MYSELF.

YOU SHOULD TRY ASKING THE GUY WITH POLKA'S FACE DIRECTLY.

Then I'll work hard to be more trustworthy.

YOU MUSTN'T PLEAD WITH SOMEONE LIKE HIM, MASTER!

NGH!! Y-YOU CAN'T DO THAT!

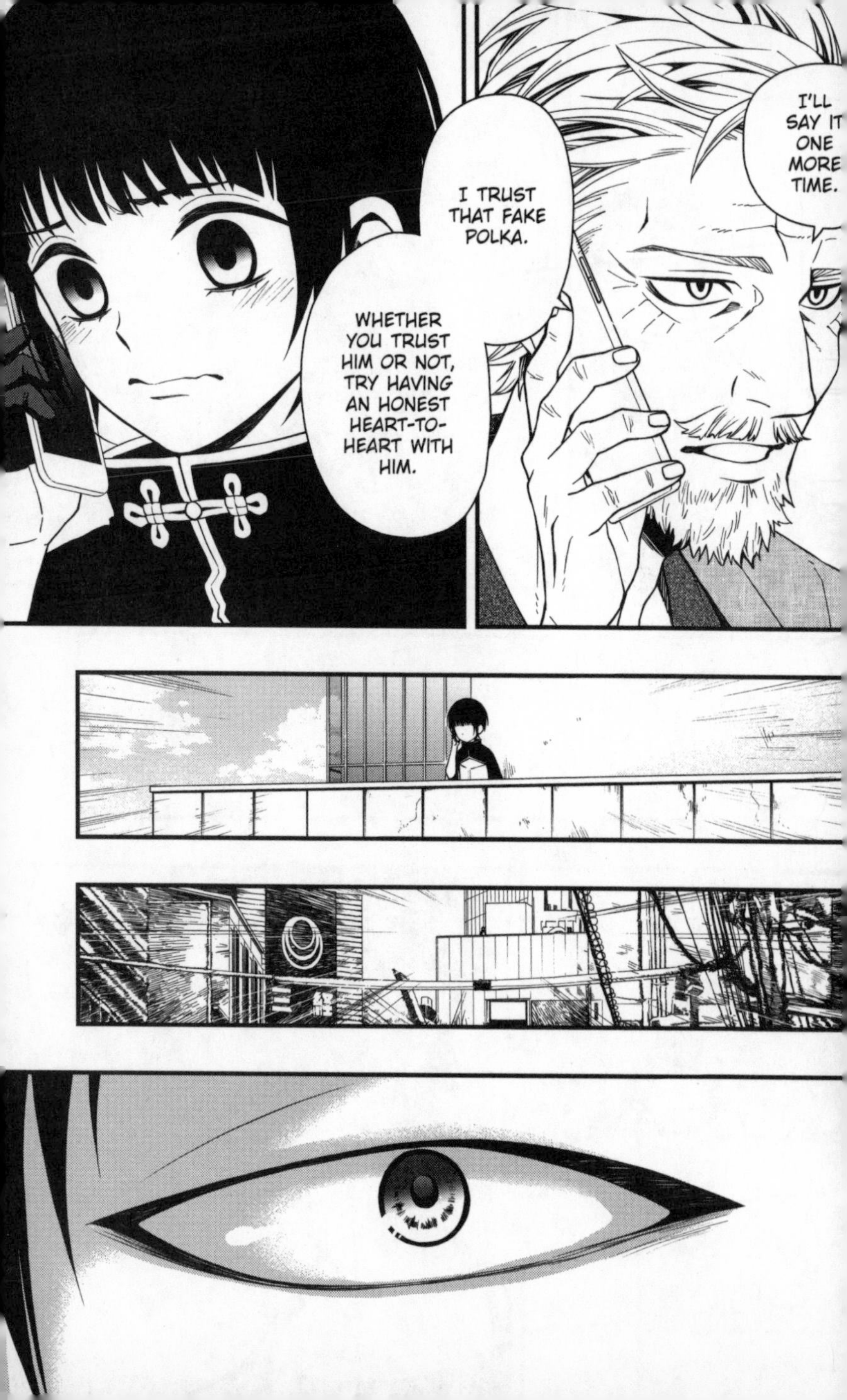
I'LL SAY IT ONE MORE TIME.
I TRUST THAT FAKE POLKA.
WHETHER YOU TRUST HIM OR NOT, TRY HAVING AN HONEST HEART-TO-HEART WITH HIM.

I JUST SAW A FAMILIAR FACE.

MY BAD.

SHINJUKU IS KURAKI'S TERRITORY, SO I'D LIKE TO KEEP FROM ATTRACTING ATTENTION, IF WE CAN.

WHAT'S THE MATTER?

SIGN: OCCUPATION, HOST.

I'M IMPRESSED. HE HAS MY RESPECT.

...HE'S STILL GOING.

EVEN THOUGH I *SHREDDED HIS LIMBS TO NOTHING...*

I SWEAR, THEY'RE AS STUBBORN AS CENTIPEDES.

THOSE HEILEI GUYS.

...NOTH-ING.

MM? WHAT'S UP, ARASE?

......IT COULDN'T BE, COULD IT?

I JUST THOUGHT I SPOTTED A FAMILIAR FACE.

UNTIL WE KNOW MORE ABOUT THIS PERSON, WE CAN'T SAY FOR SURE WHETHER THEY'RE AN ENEMY OR ALLY.

SO WHAT'S THE GAME PLAN, POLKA?

I...

...

I'LL BE LEAVING ALL THIS PARALLEL-UNIVERSE STUFF TO YOU, OKAY?

AH.

G-GOOD MORNING.

GOOD MORNING!

NOW SMILE! SMILE!

DON'T MAKE THAT FACE! NO, NO!

WHAT'S THE MATTER? WHY THE LONG FACE?

MUNI (MOOSH)

SA (SHWIP)

OH YEAH! I'VE GOT BIG NEWS! BIG NEWS!

WHAT GIVES!?

!?

PASHA (FLASH)

ZUI (LOOM)

NICE TO MEET YOU!

GEH!

"WEEKLY DRY"... "EIGHTPORT KOCHOU"... SAN?

ALLOW ME TO INTRODUCE MYSELF.

Weekly Dry **EIGHTPORT KOCHOU**

...HUH?

SHE SAYS WE'RE GOING TO BE IN THE NEWS!

...IS A WEEKLY TABLOID FOUNDED IN 1996 BY THE EDITORIAL DEPARTMENT OF ANYWHERE, INC.

WEEKLY DRY...

#37

EVERY WEEK, THEY DISTRIBUTE 220,000 COPIES, MAKING IT ONE OF THE BIGGEST NEWSPAPERS IN THE COUNTRY.

...TO LOCAL GOSSIP, THE OCCULT, AND THE LATEST GAMES.

THEY COVER EVERYTHING FROM SERIOUS POLITICAL STORIES AND THE ARTS...

IN LOVE

BIG SCOOP SAKASHITA CHEESE DIET IS A

YETI BIG-FOOT

KILLER TAKATO UEMURA TESTIFIES

NEITHER DOES THE REAL POLKA!

BUT THE CORPSE GOD KNOWS NOTHING ABOUT THAT!

WHETHER SHE'S COVERING POLITICS OR THE ARTS, SHE KNOWS NO FEAR AND HAS WRITTEN SOME FINE EXPOSÉS!

EIGHTPORT KOCHOU IS A CAPABLE JUNIOR REPORTER AT WEEKLY DRY!

CAN POLKA AND THE OTHERS KEEP THEIR COOL IN THE FACE OF THIS SURPRISE MEDIA VISIT!?

SELF-NARRATING TO ESCAPE REALITY

YOU'RE THE ONLY ONE WE CAN COUNT ON!

YOU CAN DO IT, TAKUMI. DON'T GIVE UP, TAKUMI.

THE ONLY ONE!

ONLY ONE!

ONLY ONE...

#37

THAT'S RIGHT! KEE-HEE-HEE! IT'LL BE OUR NATIONAL DEBUT!

W-WE'RE GOING TO BE IN THE NEWS??

THAT'S EXACTLY HOW A CHARACTER WHO GETS EATEN BY A SHARK IN THE SECOND ACT REACTS.

THAT'S EXACTLY HOW SOMEONE WHO HAS DONE SOMETHING REACTS...

I HAVEN'T DONE ANYTHING.

UH!

BUT, UM...

I'M INNO- CENT.

OH, THE FORTUNE-TELLING.

PHEW.

...I CAME HERE TO COVER THE PROMISING NEW FORTUNE-TELLER!

SURE, I'M CURIOUS ABOUT THIS BUSINESS WITH THE "HANDS" AND SOLITAIRE THAT'S BEEN ALL THE BUZZ SINCE THIS MORNING, BUT......

AH-HA-HA. PLEASE, RELAX.

49

SORRY ABOUT THAT. I JUST WANTED A CANDID SHOT.

OF COURSE, I WON'T ARGUE IF YOU DON'T WANT ME TO DO A STORY ON YOU.

SORRY, BUT WE CAN'T TRUST A REPORTER WHO WOULD SUDDENLY TAKE PHOTOS OF SOMEONE WITHOUT THEIR CONSENT.

カシ
(GASHI
(GRAB))

THERE ARE RUMORS ABOUT A DRONE REGULARLY FLYING AROUND THE AREA... RIGHT?

IT'D BE BAD IF AN INFORMANT WERE USING IT TO TAKE PICTURES OF PEOPLE WITHOUT THEIR CONSENT.

A DIF- FERENT STORY?

I'LL JUST COVER A DIFFERENT STORY.

SHE DID HER RESEARCH ON ME BEFORE COMING HERE!

THIS JERK—!!!

EXPOSED!
Sham Fortune-Teller Working with Former Hoodlum Informant!

YOU CAME HERE INTENDING TO EXPOSE A SHAM FORTUNE-TELLER WHO WORKS WITH AN INFORMANT, HUH?

WELL, WELL, WELL, I'VE FIGURED YOU OUT, SEE?

THE DAY THAT HAPPENS...

...THE PROBLEM IS IF SHE STARTS LOOKING INTO CLARISSA, WHO'S LENDING THIS SPACE TO POLKA.

I DON'T MIND SO MUCH IF WE'RE EXPOSED AS FRAUDS, BUT......

AAH!

WAAH!

GATA GATA (SHAKE)

GATA

GATA

GATA

GATA

...I'M SCREWED, TO PUT IT MILDLY.

......

I HAVE TO SETTLE THIS THING PEACEFULLY...

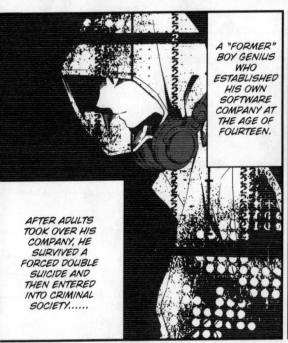

A "FORMER" BOY GENIUS WHO ESTABLISHED HIS OWN SOFTWARE COMPANY AT THE AGE OF FOURTEEN.

AFTER ADULTS TOOK OVER HIS COMPANY, HE SURVIVED A FORCED DOUBLE SUICIDE AND THEN ENTERED INTO CRIMINAL SOCIETY......

TAKUMI KURUYA... AN INFORMANT FORMERLY ASSOCIATED WITH THE GANG "SONS OF THE STYX."

...YOU'RE NOT MY TARGET THIS TIME.

YOUR LIFE COULD MAKE A GOOD STORY, BUT...

......A FORTUNE-TELLER?

WEEKLY DRY *EDITORIAL DEPARTMENT*

CHIEF EDITOR

TWO DAYS AGO

BOOKS: ANCIENT CIVILIZATIONS / SECRET DEITIES / UFO, ETC.

I'D LIKE TO DO A STORY ON THE CORPSE GOD, SO COULD I ASK FOR A WHOLE PAGE IN THE OCCULT CORNER TO COVER IT?

YES, CHIEF.

YES, THE TWO ARE RELATED!

BUT YOU WERE ON THE... SOLITAIRE CASE, WEREN'T YOU?

THE GUYS ON THE OCCULT TEAM ARE WILLING TO RUN ANYTHING, SO I PERSONALLY DON'T MIND.

...I SAW THEM POKING AROUND AT A FORTUNE-TELLER'S PLACE IN SHINJUKU.

...AND AFTER INVESTIGATING THE FIRE AT THE SHINOYAMA ESTATE—THE ONE RUMORED TO HAVE INVOLVED FIRE-BREATHING BUG...

I'VE BEEN WATCHING THE DETECTIVES INVOLVED IN THE SOLITAIRE CASE...

AND IF MY SOURCES ARE CORRECT...

...HE MAY ACTUALLY BE A MEMBER OF THE SHINOYAMA FAMILY.

HE'S A FORTUNE-TELLER CALLED "THE CORPSE GOD" WHO JUST RECENTLY OPENED FOR BUSINESS AND IS ALREADY PRETTY POPULAR......

The Best Fortune-Tellers

I KNOW THOSE DETECTIVES AREN'T THE TYPE TO WASTE TIME ON DEAD ENDS.

THAT ALONE IS PRETTY INTERESTING ALREADY...

...THE SON OF THAT WEALTHY FAMILY IS A FORTUNE-TELLER?

...AND THE RICH FAMILY'S MYSTERIOUS FORTUNE-TELLER...

SOLITAIRE'S ESCAPE...

...THE SHINOYAMA ESTATE FIRE...

THEY'RE ALL CONNECTED...!

MY TIME-HONED INTUITION AS A REPORTER IS TELLING ME.

...THE POLICE MIGHT ACTUALLY BE INVOLVED WITH THE ATTEMPTED ASSASSINATION OF SOLITAIRE...!!

AND...

THIS IS ONLY YOUR THIRD YEAR AT THE COMPANY...

YOUR TIME-HONED INTUITION...?

UH.

I LOOK FORWARD TO WORKING WITH YOU FROM NOW ON.

THANK YOU VERY MUCH!

AND WE CAN TALK COMPENSATION LATER!

DO THAT PART FIRST.

OKAY, AS LONG AS YOU RESTRICT YOUR STORY TO JUST THE FORTUNE-TELLING......

OH, NO. I WANT TO REMAIN AS OBJECTIVE AS POSSIBLE...

OKAY, SO DO YOU WANT ME TO TELL YOUR FORTUNE FIRST, KOCHOU-SAN?

NO, IT'S OKAY. MY COMPANY KNOWS TO RESPECT OTHERS' PRIVACY TOO!

HUH? BUT THE AVERAGE CLIENT WOULDN'T WANT THEIR PRIVATE WORRIES LISTENED IN ON......

THEN YOU WANT TO WATCH OTHER PEOPLE HAVING THEIR FORTUNES TOLD?

WAIT— YOU MEAN TODAY'S NOT THE ONLY DAY YOU'LL BE INVESTIGATING US?

...JUST PROMISE NOT TO HARASS THE CLIENTS CURRENTLY LINED UP, OKAY?

IF IT'S ALL RIGHT, STARTIN TOMORROW...

...I'D LIKE YOU TO MEET SOME CLIENTS THAT WE PREPARED WHO WANT THEIR FORTUNES TOLD PUBLICLY.

PEOPLE COME HERE FOR ALL SORTS OF REASONS AND SOME WOULD PREFER TO KEEP THEIR IDENTITIES HIDDEN.

WHAT A GOOD REPORTER!

SURE THING! I PROMISE I WON'T BE ANY TROUBLE.

...LET'S JUST HOPE SO.

OKAY, THEN... I GUESS I'LL GET US READY FOR BUSINESS.

JACKPOT! THIS TICKET IS REALLY PAYING OFF!

I CAN'T BELIEVE SOLITAIRE APPEARED AT THIS BUILDING THIS MORNING!

WHAT TIMING!!

AND WHY WOULD HE PULL THAT STUNT WITH ALL THOSE GAUDY HANDS IN THE MIDDLE OF THE NIGHT WHEN ALMOST NOBODY WOULD SEE?

Midnight Mystery: Flock of hand appears in Shinjuku overnight

IF MY INFORMATION'S ACCURATE, THIS FORTUNE-TELLER—

A SHINOYAMA TEAMING UP WITH AN INFORMANT TO ACT AS A FAKE FORTUNE-TELLER IS DEFINITELY SUSPICIOUS!!

AND YET, THE MOMENT I SAID I WAS HERE TO COVER HIS FORTUNE-TELLING, HE SEEMED RELIEVED!

THE CORPSE GOD'S REAL NAME IS POLKA SHINOYAMA.

58

I KNEW IT... BUT...

I KNEW IT. EVERYTHING'S CONNECTED!!

This world is a buggy program. Are you a termite. Or are you a bird eating the bug?

...WHAT IS THAT???

I HIT THE LOTTERY SO HARD, I'M ACTUALLY A LITTLE FREAKED OUT!!

SO SCARED, IN FACT, THAT I DECIDED TO PRETEND I DON'T SEE IT!!

ISN'T THAT THE LINE FIRE-BREATHING BUG LEAVES AT THE SCENES OF THEIR CRIMES?

THAT WALL THERE... IS IT SOME KIND OF PRO-FIRE-BREATHING BUG TRIBUTE?

ビクッ

BIKU (JOLT)

UM...I'VE BEEN MEANING TO ASK.

UZU

うず

BUT AS A REPORTER, I MUST ASK!!

UZU (FIDGET)

うず

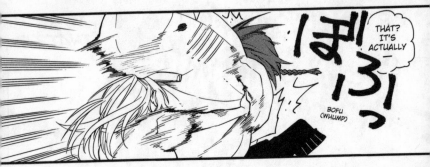

THAT? IT'S ACTUALLY

ボフ

ボフ

BOFU (WHUMP)

...YOU MEAN THAT GRAFFITI? IT WAS THERE BEFORE WE MOVED IN.

UNFORTU-NATELY, IT WON'T WASH OFF... WHAT ABOUT IT?

NOTHING TO SEE HERE. JUST OUR DAILY *SHARK WRESTLING.*

?

むぎゅ

MUGYU (SQUISH)

I DOUBT THAT.

...I SEE.

TH-THAT'S RIGHT...!?

Y... YES!

STOP IT! JUST STOP TALKING ALREADY!!

WOULD IT BE SIMPLISTIC TO CONNECT THEM NOT ONLY TO SOLITAIRE BUT TO FIRE-BREATHING BUG TOO?

~This world is a buggy program... Are you a termite!

THE WRITING LOOKS FRESH...

THE SHINO-YAMA FAMILY...

......NO, I CAN'T BE TOO CAREFUL.

...IS ALREADY AT THE CENTER OF PLENTY OF DARK RUMORS.

POLICE

Shinoyama Family Victim of Arso...

KOKURI (NOD)

こくり

SO ARE YOU OKAY...

...NEZU?

こくり

KOKURI

...SO LET ME GET THIS STRAIGHT.

FROM WHAT YOU SAW, THOSE "THINGS" WEREN'T THE WORK OF SOLITAIRE?

OF COURSE, AT THIS POINT, I CAN'T IMAGINE YOU'D BE HURT JUST FROM FALLING OFF A BUILDING.

BOTH SOLITAIRE AND MY OLD MAN'S GUARDS HAVE THEIR EYE ON YOU.

YOU CAN TAKE A LITTLE TIME OFF NOW.

I SEE...

GO (RUMBLE)

GO

GO

AND NEXT WEEK...

...YOU'LL BE BUSY WITH YOUR *MAIN JOB*, RIGHT?

......

NO NEED TO THANK ME. JUST DON'T GET TOO BADLY BEAT UP DOING YOUR OTHER JOB.

AH. THAT PAUSE JUST NOW... WAS BECAUSE HE WAS THANKING HIM.

ペコリ
PEKORI (BOW)

TAIPEI.

YES, SIR.

...AND GO AFTER SOLITAIRE.

GET IN TOUCH WITH THE MAIN FORCES OF THE LEI FAMILY...

I'M CURIOUS TO SEE WHAT HE KNOWS ABOUT POLKA.

TRY TO BRING HIM IN ALIVE.

YOU WANT HIM DEAD?

YOU CAN HANG AROUND NEAR THE BUILDING POLKA'S IN.

AS YOU WISH.

AND I WANT TO THANK HIM FOR THE DROP IN SHINOYAMA SECURITY'S STOCK PRICES.

MM-HM, YOU GOT IT.

YOU SUPPORT HIM FROM BEHIND THE SCENES BY PROVIDING INTEL.

BAO.

MM-HM?

WE ALREADY LET THEM INVESTIGATE US, BUT THEY'RE PROBABLY FOLLOWING OUR MOVEMENTS.

THE POLICE ARE DEVOTING A LOT OF THEIR MEN TO THE SOLITAIRE CASE.

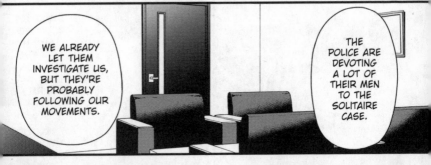

THEY'RE A REAL NEST OF VIPERS.

...DON'T LET YOUR GUARD DOWN AROUND THE POLICE.

SIGN: METROPOLITAN POLICE DEPARTMENT

THERE'S NO TELLING WHAT THEY'RE UP TO.

SO IT'S THE SHINO-YAMAS......

I THOUGHT I SMELLED A NOSY RAT......

Takeru Shinoyama

DEPENDING ON WHAT HAPPENS, I MAY HAVE TO ASK HIM TO WITHDRAW.

AND I THINK THERE'S AN EVEN MORE INTERESTING CONNECTION THAN I'D IMAGINED HERE.

YES.

I'LL BE ABLE TO START INTERVIEWING TOMORROW.

LEAVE IT TO ME, CHIEF!

You going to be okay? No matter what, your story'll run in the occult section, so don't overdo it...

...THAT IN THIS BUILDING...

MY INTUITION'S TELLING ME...

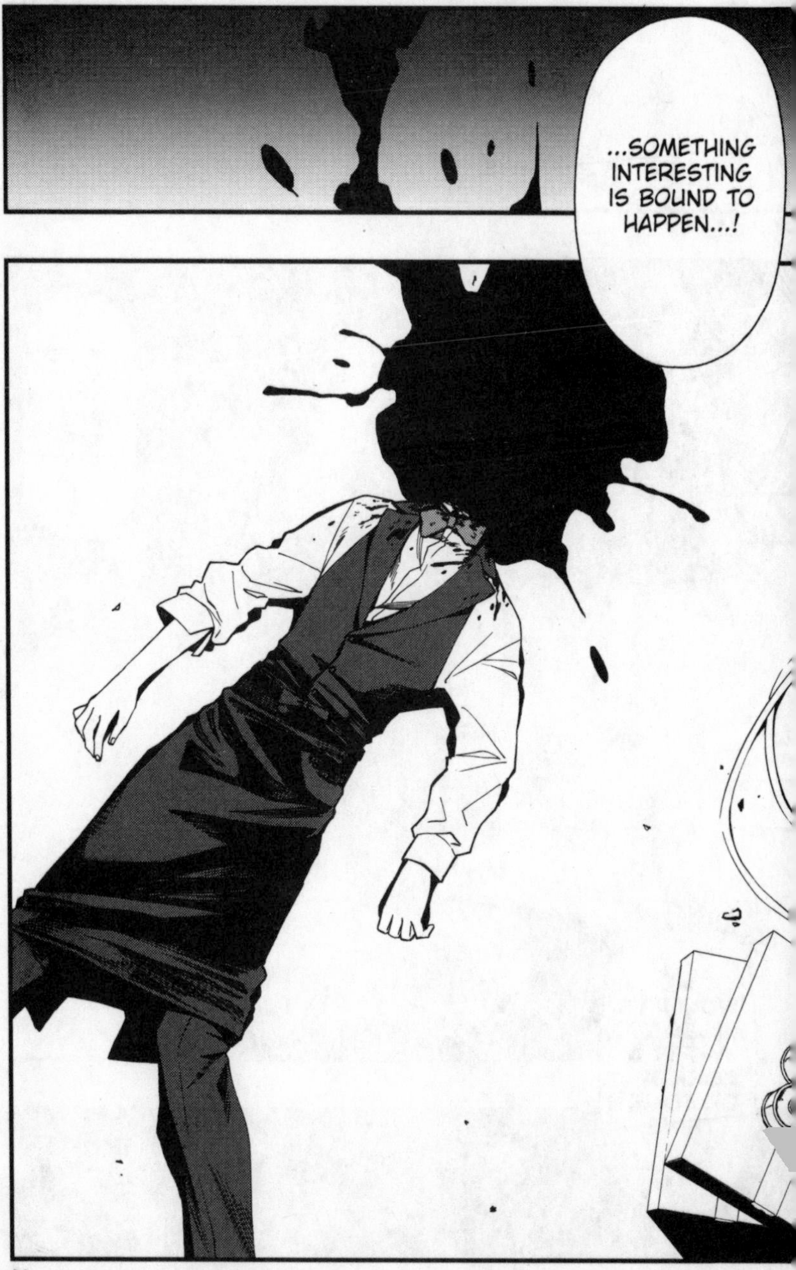
...SOMETHING INTERESTING IS BOUND TO HAPPEN...!

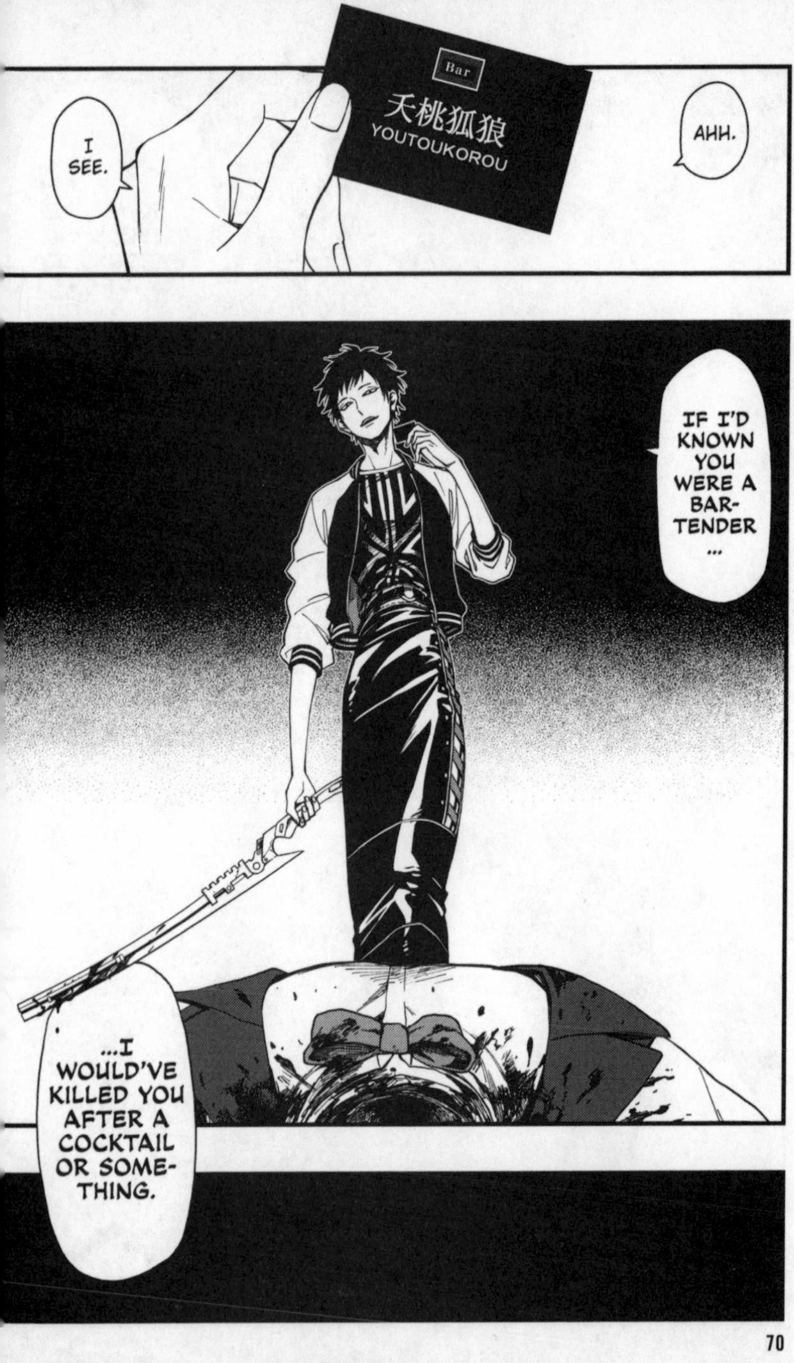
Bar
天桃狐狼
YOUTOUKOROU
AHH.
I SEE.
IF I'D KNOWN YOU WERE A BAR-TENDER...
...I WOULD'VE KILLED YOU AFTER A COCKTAIL OR SOME-THING.

I...

I THOUGHT I WAS GOING TO DIE...

#38

HOW COULD NISHIDA MISS WORK WITHOUT CALLING IN DURING OUR BUSIEST TIME...?

THANKS TO HIM, I HAD TO TEND THE BAR ALL BY MYSELF TODAY!! WITHOUT ANY BREAKS!

UGH! NO MOOORE!

YOU'LL BE GETTING A BONUS FOR ALL YOUR HARD WORK, SO I HOPE YOU CAN FORGIVE ME.

GOOD JOB TODAY.

A BONUS!?

PAAA- (GLOW)

ぽん
PON
(PAT)

A BONUS... NOW I CAN BUY A BUNCH OF PHOTO BOOKS...!

THANK YOU SO MUCH!

AND HERE'S SOMETHING FROM ME. ON THE HOUSE.

HE'S GETTING A DRINK FROM CLARISSA...

LUCKYYY.

...CHECK IN ON NISHIDA-KUN'S APARTMENT FOR ME?

CAN SOME-ONE...

...MAKE IT A GROUP OF TWO OR MORE.

...JUST TO BE SAFE...

#38

... HIGURO-SAN.

I TELL YA, THE WORLD'S ENDING...

I MEAN, EVEN I'M HAVING TO ACT AS A MIDDLEMAN IN SHIBUYA.

WHAT ERA HASN'T BEEN "THE END" OF SOMETHING?

STILL, I HONESTLY CAN'T BELIEVE WHAT SOLITAIRE SAID WAS RIGHT ON THE MARK.

FINE, THEN IT'S JUST GETTING BETTER AND BETTER.

I THINK IT'S ON A ONE-WAY TRACK TO DETERIORATION, YOU KNOW?

...AND THE CLIENT WHO ASKED THIS OF ME...

BETWEEN THE POLICE'S ASSASSINATION ATTEMPT ON SOLITAIRE...

LIVE

IF IT MEANS HAVING TO RELY ON THE GIRLS, I'D RATHER LIVE WITH A HUNDRED THIEVES.

AGAKURA? AS IF!

WHY NOT YOUR FAMILY?

WHAT SHOULD I DO? I CAN'T TRUST THE POLICE ANYMORE.

WHO CAN I TURN TO IF A THIEF BREAKS INTO MY HOME?

THIS WAY.

...YEAH, I GUESS I CAN UNDERSTAND THAT.

GACHA (KCHAK)

75

THAT BUILDING'S UNDER SURVEIL-LANCE.

THERE'S DRONES FLYING AROUND IT TOO, SO IT'S NOT SAFE.

THAT'S WHY...

AREN'T WE GOING TO THE BUILDING SOLITAIRE SHOWED UP AT YESTERDAY?

VIA THE ROOFTOPS?

...IT'S BEEN FIVE YEARS...

...BUT HOPEFULLY, THE PASSAGE IS STILL INTACT.

...WE'RE GOING TO USE THIS BUILD-ING...

...AND CARRY THAT IN THROUGH THE BASEMENT.

IF NOT FOR YOU GUYS, A LITTLE WEAKLING LIKE ME WOULD BE TOTALLY SCREWED...

COME ON!

HONESTLY, THOUGH, UNLIKE KURAKI-SAN'S GUYS IN SHINJUKU I'M NOT MUCH LIKED BY THE UNDERBELLY OF SOCIETY.

AGAKURA-SAN'S PEOPLE ARE REALLY HELPING ME OUT.

IF YOU FAIL, THEY'LL STAB YOU IN THE BACK RATHER THAN BACK YOU UP.

OUR SPONSORS HAVE A LOT OF CLOUT, BUT I'M JUST A JUNIOR MEMBER OF THE ORGANIZATION.

LAST GIRL I BROUGHT FOR YOU, YOU BROKE, AND I HAD TO DUMP HER BODY IN THE MOUNTAINS.

BRING THAT GIRL HERE NEXT TIME.

WHO'RE YOU GUYS?

ZA
(SHFF)

OOOO

YOU'VE GOT IT ROUGH, HIGURO-SAN.

AH...BUT THIS PLACE DOESN'T BELONG TO YOU GUYS, RIGHT?

YOU SHOULDN'T REALLY BE HANGING OUT HERE...

H-HE'S HUGE...

GET LOST, DUDES.

MY HANDS ARE FULL, SO OF COURSE THEY WOULD BLUFF.

YOU LOOK LIKE SUCH A WEAKLING, HIGURO-SAN.

WOW. THEY'RE PICKING A FIGHT WITH US.

MISTER. HEY, MISTER.

WHY DON'T YOU DONATE SOME MONEY TO OUR CAUSE?

HUH?

GASHI (GRAB)

DON'T YOU DARE IGNORE US!

YEAH, WELL, THE TRUTH IS I AM WEAK.

SHUT UP, YOU HEAR ME?

UUUH... I'D LOVE TO ASK YOU A QUESTION FIRST—

PAN (SMACK)

DO YOU HAVE ANY PULL?

PASA (FLOP)

...GUYS.

I BELIEVE CONNEC-TIONS...

...ARE LOVE.

HUH?

PULL. YOU KNOW.

LIKE CONTACTS.

CON-NEC-TIONS.

...ARE YOU LOVED?

WHAT I WANT TO KNOW IS...

???

WHAT'S THIS GUY TALKING ABOUT?

ARE ANY OF YOUR FRIENDS OR FAMILY MEMBERS POLITICIANS OR BIG-SHOT COPS?

ANY LEGENDARY MERCENARIES? SUPER- HEROES? WORLD- RENOWNED KARATE MASTERS?

YOU HAVE ANYONE WHO LOVES YOU SO MUCH, THEY'D RISK THEIR LIFE FOR YOU?

EVEN AN ORDINARY PERSON WILL DO.

IN THAT CASE, IF WE KILL HIM, WE'LL BE DOIN' THE COPS A FAVOR, EH?

HE'S TRIPPING, FOR SURE.

...IS HE ON SOMETHING?

SO THERE'S NOBODY IN YOUR LIVES LIKE THAT?

AS A MATTER OF FACT...

...I DO.

NO, THERE ISN'T, JACKASS!

WHAT ABOUT YOU? I HOPE YOU HAVE A FRIEND IN THE FUNERAL BUSINESS.

GRANTED, THEY PRACTICE WITHOUT A LICENSE.

HUH?

BRGHNH?

PASHU (PSHH)

HRBABH...?

BOTA (DRIP)

AH...

NH...

HUH?

UH...

...A GREAT CONNECTION.

AND THEY ARE...

BOSHU

BOSHU
(BSHHT)

BOSHU

THEY'LL DISPOSE OF YOU GUYS...

...WITHOUT LEAVING A TRACE BEHIND.

WOULDN'T IT HAVE BEEN QUICKER TO JUST SHOOT THEM IN THEIR HEADS AT THIS RANGE?

GUH!

UNDER-STAND WHAT?

I FIGURED THEY'D WANT TO UNDERSTAND BEFORE THEY DIE.

IF YOU GUYS HAD CONTACTS, I WOULDN'T KILL YOU.

HFF...

DO YOU KNOW WHY YOU'RE GOING TO DIE?

KHFF...

IF YOU GUYS HAD SOME DANGEROUS CONTACTS IN YOUR ARSENAL, I WOULD'VE HESITATED TO UPSET THEM.

キョロ
KYORO

キョロ
(GLANCE)
KYORO

HAAH...

YEP. NOBODY THERE.

CON-TACTS ARE LOVE.

BUT WHEN THAT LOVE TURNS INTO HATE, IT MAKES TAKING OUT TARGETS TRICKY.

PEOPLE OFTEN SAY THAT LOVE SAVES THE WORLD.

I BELIEVE CONNECTIONS ARE THE LOVE AN INDIVIDUAL HAS FOR SOCIETY.

BUT YOU GUYS HAVE NO LOVE.

SO NOBODY'S GOING TO SAVE YOU.

I'M FORRY... F...FPARE ME...

N... NO.

YOU'RE WASTING YOUR BULLETS, MAN!

AH HA HA HA!

BOSHU CBSHHT

BOSHU

BOSHU

BOSHU

IT'D SUCK IF WE WERE CAUGHT.

DANG... I DIDN'T WANT TO ATTRACT ATTENTION IN SHINJUKU...

HYUCK HYUCK!

I'M NOT STRONG LIKE YOU GUYS.

SO OVERKILL IS JUST WHAT I NEED.

OKAY.

I'LL HAVE MY "UNDERTAKER" FRIEND CLEAN UP THIS PLACE LATER.

TRUE. NOW BE CAREFUL NOT TO STEP IN THE BLOOD.

HYOI (CHOP)

WHAT IF THEY'RE THE SONS OF SOME SUPER-POWERFUL POLITICIAN OR SOME-THING?

WHAT IF THEY WERE LYING?

TOLD YOU THE WORLD WAS ENDING.

SEE?

I'D JUST GO INTO HIDING FOR A WHILE AGAIN.

I'LL DEAL WITH IT WHEN THE TIME COMES.

...IS FREELY ROAMING THE STREETS.

AFTER ALL, A LOWLIFE LIKE YOU...

EVEN THIS WILL COME TO A CLOSE SOON.

THAT'S WHY IT'S ALWAYS "THE END."

THIS WORLD IS ON THE BRINK OF A NEW DAWN.

EVEN WHEN IT CAME TO THOSE HOOLI-GANS.

IN ANY CASE, YOU SURE ARE CONCERNED ABOUT CONNEC-TIONS.

HMMM...

I MANAGED TO GET AWAY, BUT... IN THE END...

...AN *ENTIRE ORGANIZA-TION* WAS DECIMATED.

IT'S AN OLD STORY, BUT...

...SOME TIME AGO, SOMEONE I MEDDLED WITH HAD AN ESPECIALLY DANGEROUS ALLY ON HIS SIDE...

AND IF SOLITAIRE CAN DISGUISE HIMSELF ANYWAY, THIS COULD ALL BE FOR NOTHING.

MAYBE.

DANG, THERE'S SO MANY PEOPLE ON SHINJUKU'S SURVEILLANCE CAMERAS, IT'S MAKING MY HEAD SPIN...

WHAT IS IT?

WHOA.

NOTHING. IT'S JUST SOMETHING FROM THIS MORNING'S FOOTAGE.

DOES HE REALIZE POLKA SHINOYAMA KNOWS ABOUT THAT MARK?

EITHER WAY, I NEED TO SEE POLKA SHINOYAMA ONE MORE TIME......

BUT KNOWING SOLITAIRE'S PERSONALITY, CHANCES ARE HE'LL RETURN TO THAT BUILDING... THE QUESTION IS, "WHY?"

WOW, YOU'RE RIGHT...

HE'S EASILY OVER TWO METERS TALL......

TALL?

YOU SAID IT.

I WAS JUST SURPRISED TO SEE SUCH A RIDICULOUSLY TALL GUY.

....!?

SO I WASN'T MISTAKEN...!

ARASE?

HEY! WHAT'S THE BIG IDEA, ARASE?

ひょい
HYOI
(YANK)

HUH!?

I'M TALKING ABOUT THE GUY NEXT TO HIM.

NO, I DON'T KNOW HIM.

HM? YOU KNOW THIS TALL GUY?

YEP. HE WAS AFFILIATED WITH AN ORGANIZATION I TOOK OUT A FEW YEARS AGO.

OH... ISN'T THAT...?

...BUT EVEN NOW, I'M CONVINCED HE WAS THE ONE PULLING ALL THE STRINGS.

THE INVESTIGATION WAS CANCELED BEFORE I COULD BRING HIM IN......

I'M SORRY, BUT WE DON'T HAVE TIME FOR UNRELATED CASES...

LOOK, ARASE, WE HAVE TO FOCUS ON FINDING SOLITAIRE.

OH, THIS ISN'T FROM THE SOLITAIRE CASE...

AND YOU WERE IN A DIFFERENT DEPARTMENT AT THE TIME...

WELL, NOW...... I DON'T RECOGNIZE THIS FACE.

BUT HE IS RELATED.

OH YEAH! YOU MENTIONED BEFORE...

......!

HE'S INDIRECTLY CONNECTED TO POLKA SHINOYAMA.

THAT GUY POLKA SHINOYAMA IS FRIENDS WITH...!

BUT DON'T YOUR FORTUNE-TELLING OUTFITS COVER MOST OF YOUR FACES?

NEE-HEE...

KEE-HEE!

IF SHE'S GOING TO DO A STORY ON US, A SMILE'S VERY IMPORTANT!

IT'S NOT AS IF I'M MAKING NO PROGRESS.

BUT PEOPLE WHO KNOW SOMETHING ABOUT THAT MARK ARE CONTACTING ME...

EVERY-THING'S SUDDENLY GOTTEN SO BUSY...

PHEW.

JACKET: WATCH OUT FOR FIRES

DON'T GET TOO WORKED UP, NOW.

...I'M COUNTING ON YOU, TAKUMI-KUN.

YES...

I'M INNOCENT.

TH-THAT'S RIGHT...!?

OH NO! OH NO!

NICE AND EASY...

BUT FIRST, WE HAVE TO ENSURE THIS STORY GOES WITHOUT A HITCH.

The first time he came was for reconnaissance. The second time he visited to confirm the link between that mark and Polka.

KA (TAKK)

KA

KA

But we don't know what Solitaire's aims are.

ARASE AND IWANOME.

SOLITAIRE AND FIRE-BREATHING BUG.

AND NOW, THIS REPORTER TURNS UP.

DON'T SUPPOSE YOU FEEL LIKE SHARING WHAT YOU KNOW ABOUT THAT MARK WITH US, DO YOU?

WORSE, FIRE-BREATHING BUG IS INVOLVED IN THIS TOO.

...

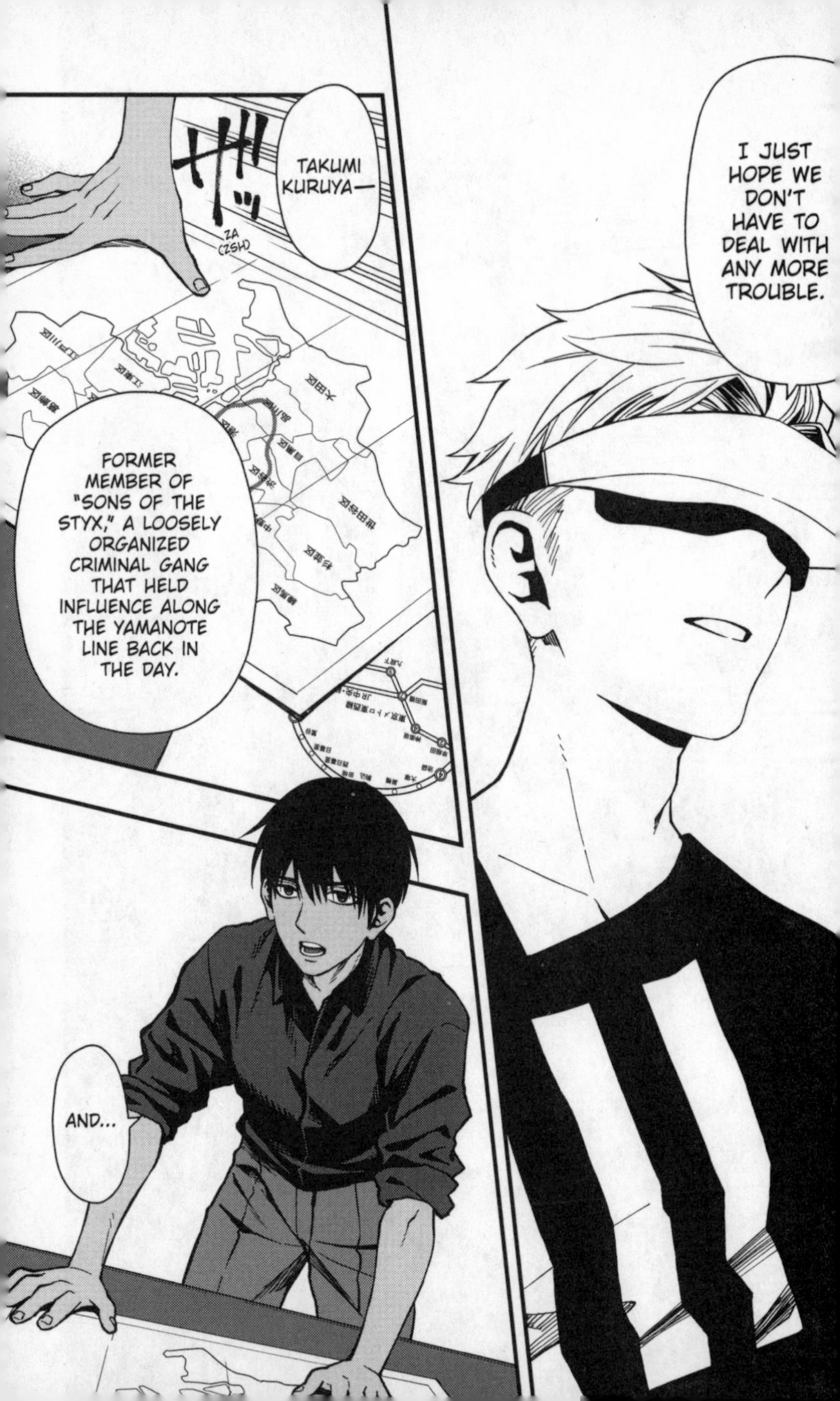

I JUST HOPE WE DON'T HAVE TO DEAL WITH ANY MORE TROUBLE.
ザッ
ZA (ZSH)
TAKUMI KURUYA—
FORMER MEMBER OF "SONS OF THE STYX," A LOOSELY ORGANIZED CRIMINAL GANG THAT HELD INFLUENCE ALONG THE YAMANOTE LINE BACK IN THE DAY.
AND...

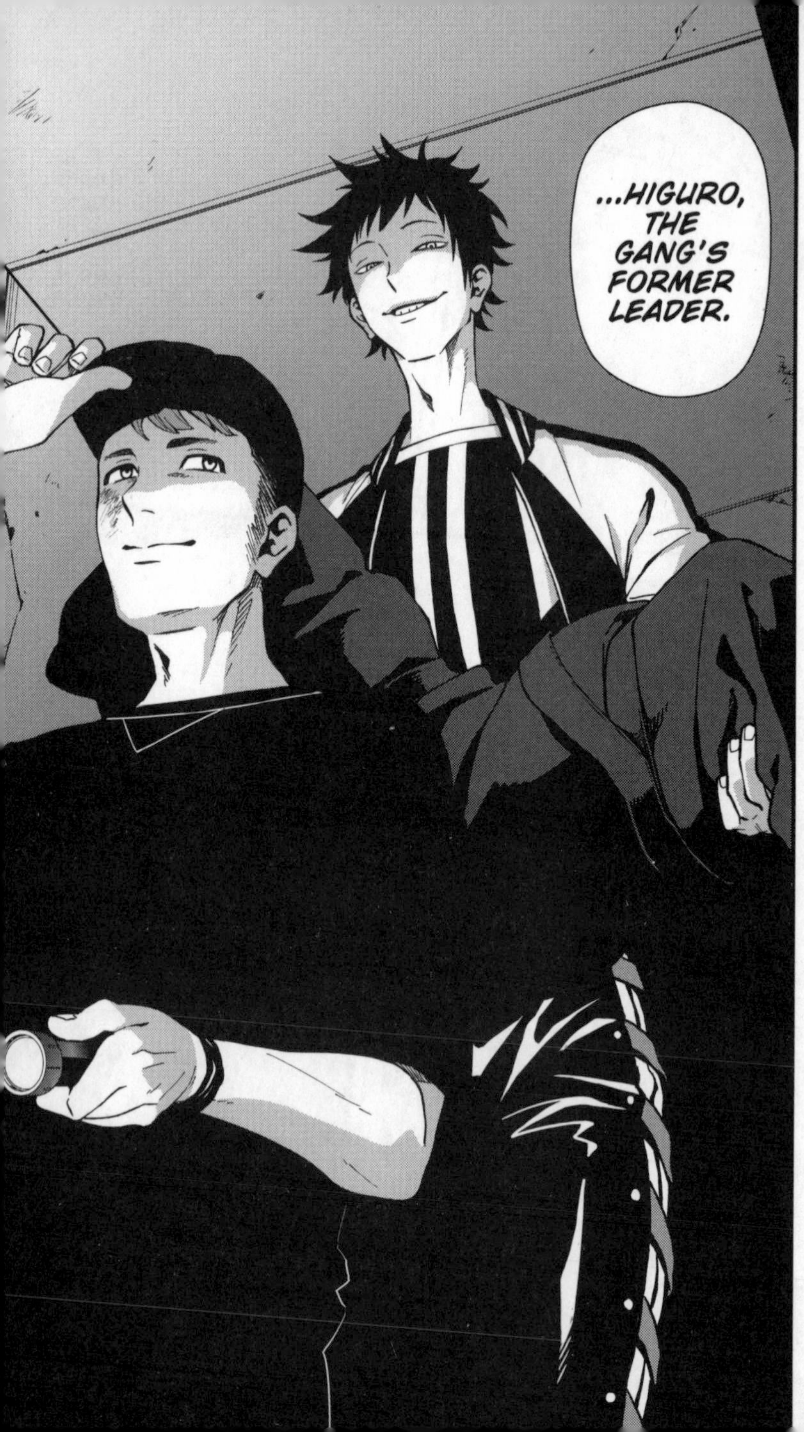
...HIGURO, THE GANG'S FORMER LEADER.

WHY AM I HERE...?

HUH?

I REMEMBER GETTING A WEIRD PHONE CALL, AND THEN...

WHAT WAS I DOING AGAIN?

OH, THAT'S RIGHT.

I NEED TO GET BACK TO THE BAR.

#39

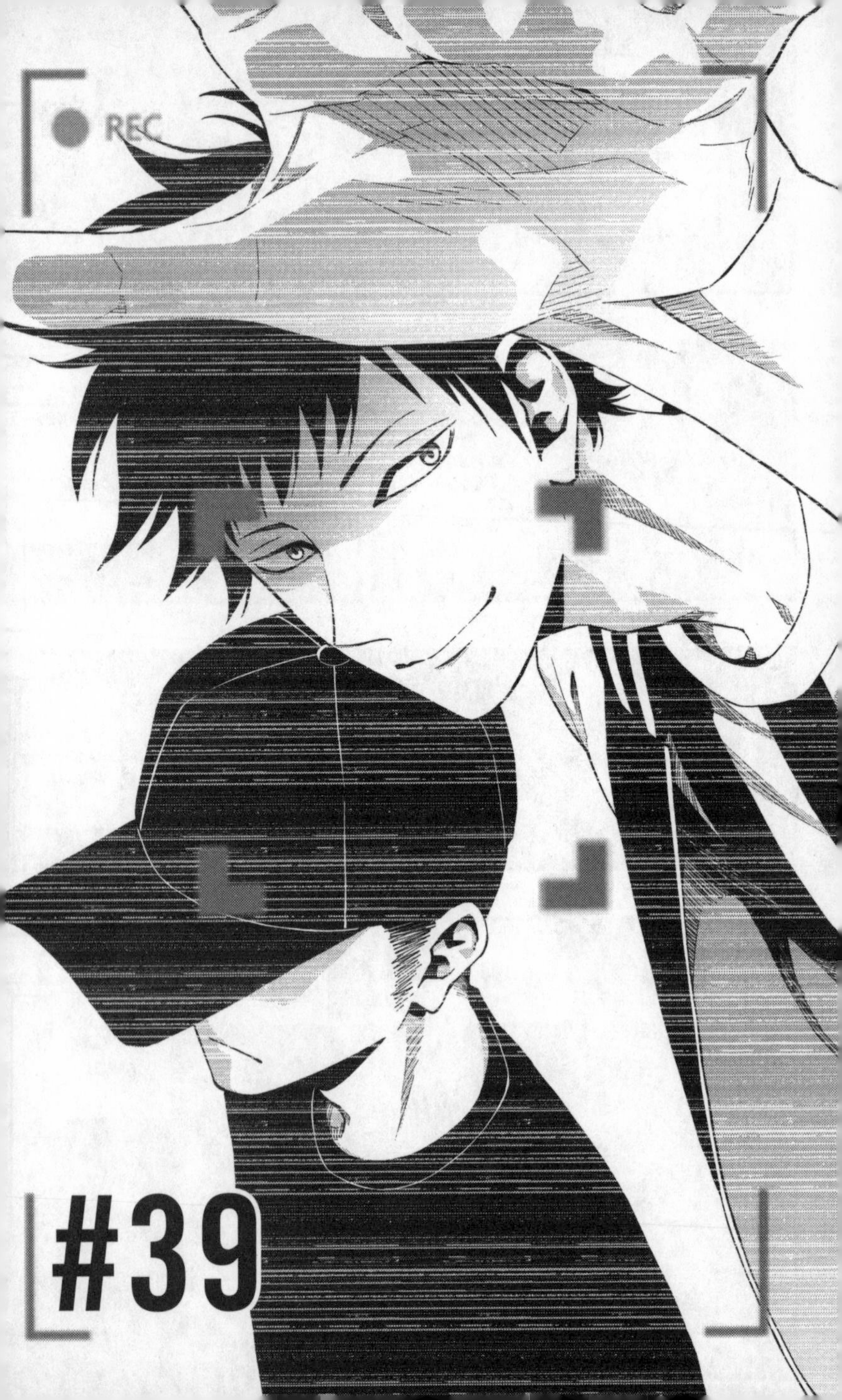
REC
#39

UGH.

I FEEL SO DIZZY.

WHERE'D I LEAVE MY PHONE...?

WHAT TIME IS IT, EVEN...?

I GUESS HIS SHIFT'S ALREADY OVER.

AH!

UH-OH. THERE'S URAI.

HEY, URAI.

EARTH TO URAI!

COME ON, URAI. WHO'S MANNING THE BAR?

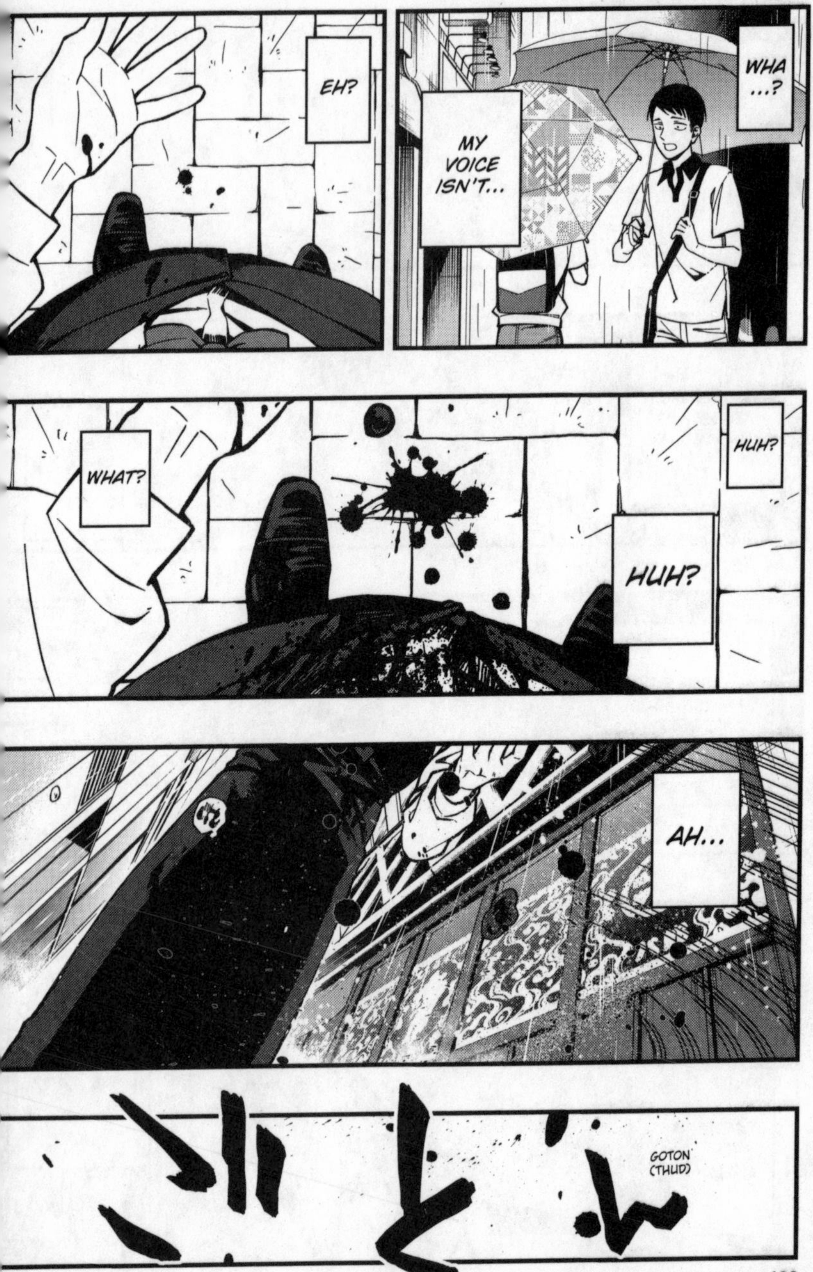
WHA ...?
MY VOICE ISN'T...
EH?
HUH?
HUH?
WHAT?
AH...
GOTON (THUD)

I REMEM-BER...

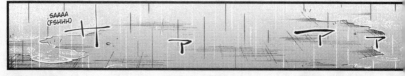

SAAAA (FSHHH)

SIGN: IMPROVE YOUR LUCK / FORTUN.

THANK YOU FOR LETTING ME SIT IN ON YOUR NEXT SESSION!

CERTAINLY.

THE PLEASURE'S ALL MINE.

IT WAS VERY KIND OF YOU TO GIVE US A THIRTY-MINUTE WINDOW BEFORE YOU OPEN! THANK YOU VERY MUCH!

TODAY, I'LL BE BRINGING IN *AROUND TWO PEOPLE* TO HAVE THEIR FORTUNES TOLD...

...BY THE WAY.

I'M MORE THAN HAPPY TO HELP PEOPLE SEE THE LAWS OF THE WORLD FROM A DIFFERENT ANGLE.

OH, IT'S NO TROUBLE AT ALL.

WHY DO YOU SUPPOSE SOLITAIRE SHOWED UP AT THIS BUILDING?

FROM WHAT I UNDERSTAND, HE WISHES FOR WHAT YOU MIGHT CALL "SUPERNATURAL PHENOMENA"...

PERHAPS... SOMETHING GUIDED HIM HERE.

THOUGH I DON'T KNOW IF I WOULD QUALIFY IN HIS EYES...AS A SUPERNATURAL PHENOMENON.

THEN HE MAY HAVE COME HERE AFTER HEARING THE RUMORS ABOUT ME.

OUR OFFICE EVEN WROTE AN ARTICLE ABOUT IT.

YES. HE'S AFTER REAL GHOSTS AND SUPERNATURAL POWERS AND THE LIKE...THAT'S WHAT HE SAYS, AT LEAST, AND IT'S CERTAINLY CAUSED QUITE A STIR.

...IT'S ALL VERY ORDINARY TO ME.

SINCE *SEEING THINGS* IS MY EVERYDAY LIFE...

...MEAN-ING?

OH WELL. IT'S NOT LIKE MY REAL AIM HERE IS HIS FORTUNE-TELLING.

HE'S MUCH CALMER THAN HE WAS YESTER-DAY...

OF COURSE, HE DID SAY HE USED TO HAVE TO PUT ON A SIMILAR ACT WITH THE NOBILITY AND MERCHANTS...

WHOA... HE MANAGED TO GET THROUGH THAT...

...I'D LOVE FOR YOU TO TELL THE FORTUNE OF THE PERSON I'VE BROUGHT.

ALL RIGHT, THEN...

I'LL "SEE" WHAT I CAN DO.

GOOD.

GACHA
(KCHAK)

THANKS...
FOR
HAVING
ME?

UH...
HELLO.

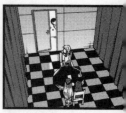

THIS IS
A-SAN,
YOUR
AVERAGE
CITIZEN!

I FOUND
HIM IN THE
NEIGHBOR-
HOOD.

WE
KNOW
THIS
GUY...

HOW DID I GET INTO THIS MESS!?

CRAP, CRAP, CRAP.

WHAT'S HE DOING ...!?

HM? YOU KNOW HIM?

HE'S A BARTENDER AT CLARISSA'S PLACE!

I FIGURED IT'D BE LIKE SAMPLING THE NEWEST FLAVOR OF BUBBLE TEA OR SOMETHING...!

BOBA

I CAME WITH HER BECAUSE SHE SAID IT WAS JUST FOR A MINOR STORY......

PRETTY PLEASE!

WHA —?

HUH?

SIR? EXCUSE ME, SIR.

WOULD YOU BE INTERESTED IN A LITTLE GIG?

CRUMBLES UNDER PRESSURE

GO GO (CRUMBLE) GO ゴ ゴ ゴ GO ゴ GO

SO HOW DID I WIND UP HERE, GETTING MY FORTUNE TOLD BY POLKA-KUN!?

...I'VE WALKED INTO A TRAP!?

URAI FILTER

DON'T TELL ME...

ばっ

BA (WHIP)

LET'S SEE HOW HE REACTS.

THIS GUY'S AFFILIATED WITH THE OWNER OF THIS BUILDING...

HEH-HEH-HEH...... FIRST, WE START WITH A QUICK JAB.

OH. HE... DOESN'T REMEMBER ME.

?

UM... GOOD TO SEE YOU.

AH.

?

HUH? THEN HOW ABOUT MISAKI-CHAN...!?

BA (WHIP)

...I'LL JUST PRETEND THIS IS OUR FIRST TIME MEETING.

...NICE TO MEET YOU.

LEAVES ZERO IMPRESSION

AND HE CAN'T TALK ABOUT ANYTHING INVOLVING CLARISSA'S BAR IN FRONT OF A JOURNALIST.

WHAT DO I DO? WHAT DO I DO?

NOT LIKE I HAVE ANY INTERESTING DATA ON HIM THAT COULD BE USED FOR A READING ANYWAY.

I GUESS I'LL KEEP MY MOUTH SHUT.

THEY DON'T RECOGNIZE HIM...? GUYS...

BUT WITH MISAKI-CHAN HERE AND KURUYA-KUN PROBABLY WATCHING FROM SOME CAMERA, IF WORD OF THIS GOT BACK TO THE BAR...

MMNH!

I WANT TO COMPLAIN ABOUT WORK! JUST LET IT ALL OUT!

UH, TROU-BLING ME?

LET US BEGIN... IS ANYTHING TROUBLING YOU?

RAH!

WAAH!

...I'D BE SCREWED, TO PUT IT MILDLY.

SU (PALE)

A-AS A MATTER OF FACT, MY NECK'S BEEN REALLY STIFF LATELY...

UH, UMM... SOMETHING TROUBLING ME... SOMETHING TROUBLING ME...

? ?

...... BUT OF COURSE.

NO, NO! I DIDN'T COME HERE TO GET A CHIROPRACTIC ADJUSTMENT!

ACTUALLY, MY COWORKER SKIPPED WORK AND WENT OFF SOMEWHERE.

I WAS WONDERING IF YOU MIGHT BE ABLE TO DIVINE WHERE HE WENT...OR SOMETHING LIKE THAT.

AH. UM... OH YEAH!

IS THIS COWORKER OF YOURS... SOMEONE IMPORTANT TO YOU?

......

I WOULDN'T SAY HE'S LIKE FAMILY, BUT...

...WELL, I GUESS HE'S A FRIEND I CAN TALK OPENLY WITH, SO... YEAH...

HUH? NO, WELL... IT'S NOT A MATTER OF HIM BEING IMPORTANT TO ME...

HOLD ON A SEC...

HUH?

NO WAY.

WE'RE HERE TO REPORT ON OUR VISIT TO NISHIDA-SAN'S PLACE.

IN FACT, IT LOOKS LIKE HE EVEN MADE IT AS FAR AS THIS BUILDING.

THERE WERE DEFINITE INDICATIONS HE DID INDEED LEAVE HIS HOME.

WE ALSO CHECKED THE BUILDING'S CAMERAS, AND THERE'S FOOTAGE OF HIM LEAVING IN A HURRY BEFORE HIS SHIFT ENDED, WITH HIS UNIFORM STILL ON.

THERE ARE SIGNS HE CHANGED INTO HIS WORK UNIFORM.

AND A WITNESS SAW HIM ENTERING THE CHANGING ROOM.

HUH? REALLY?

NISHIDA WAS HERE.

...HE STEPPED OUT WITHOUT TELLING ANYONE?

...MAYBE HE GOT A CALL?

HE COULD'VE AT LEAST SAID SOME- THING.

...THE TIMING OF ALL THIS BUGS ME, THOUGH.

...NISHIDA-KUN CERTAINLY HAS A DARK AND SHADY PAST.

SO IF SOMEONE USED THAT TO THREATEN HIM, IT WOULDN'T BE UNREASONABLE FOR HIM TO LEAVE WITHOUT NOTICE LIKE THAT.

IF IT'S SOME PERSONAL DRAMA HE WAS INVOLVED IN, THAT'S ONE THING...YOU REAP WHAT YOU SOW......

ARE YOU SAYING HE WAS KIDNAPPED? WHAT FOR?

YOU'RE IMPLYING POLKA-KUN'S INVOLVED?

Flock of Hands Appear
Shinjuku in Dead of Night

BUT FOR IT TO COME AT THE SAME TIME AS THIS DOES GIVE ME CAUSE FOR CONCERN.

THE ONLY BARTENDER WHO DOES IS...

NO, NISHIDA-KUN DOESN'T KNOW ANYTHING ABOUT POLKA-KUN.

LIKE, MAYBE NISHIDA'S BEEN CAPTURED AND IS BEING TORTURED TO SPILL WHAT HE KNOWS ABOUT POLKA-KUN?

EEEK!

WHY DID THEY CALL ME IN HERE!?

CHAPTER 3 (HE WAS THERE.)

...YOU'RE KIDDING ME, RIGHT? I KNOW POLKA-KUN'S A "NECRO-MANCER."

I FOUND THAT OUT THE FIRST TIME I SAW HIM IN THIS BUILDING...

IT CAN'T BE...

.... BUT OF COURSE.

MY NECK'S BEEN REALLY STIFF LATELY...

AND JUDGING BY WHAT POLKA-KUN JUST SAID...

YOUR FRIEND...

...MAY WELL HAVE GOTTEN MIXED UP IN SOME SERIOUS TROUBLE.

PLEASE-EASE-EASE-EASE TELL-ELL-ELL-ELL HIM-IM-IM-IM-IM...

YOU CAN SEE-EE-EE-EE-EE ME-EE-EE-EEE?

ZOKU (CHILLS)

SOME-ONE-ONE-ONE-ONE KILLED-ILLED-ILLED-ILLED ME-EE-EE-EE-EE.

AND...... THE MEAT OF THE FORTUNE HE'S GIVING IS PRETTY WEIRD...

WHAT... KIND OF REACTION IS THIS?

...?

IF THIS KID'S ONLY RANDOMLY GUESSING, HE'S RISKING LOSING HIS CREDIBILITY...

ISN'T HE SUPPOSED TO KEEP IT VAGUE AND NON-COMMITTAL AT FIRST?

TO BRING UP HIS FRIEND BEING MIXED UP IN SOME SERIOUS TROUBLE SO EARLY ON IN THE SESSION...

SO JUST WHAT IN THE HECK IS GOING ON HERE...?

HAVE THEY ALREADY MET BEFORE?

NO, IN THAT CASE, THEY'D BE GOING ABOUT THIS MUCH MORE NATURALLY...

SAKU
(SHUNK)

...NOW, THEN.

LET'S HOPE, THIS TIME...

...THEY'RE ABLE TO FIND IT EASILY.

CAR: METROPOLITAN POLICE DEPARTMENT

WHAT IS IT?

CLARISSA, WE HAVE ADDITIONAL INFORMATION ON NISHIDA-SAN.

......

THE POLICE ARE HERE, AREN'T THEY?

CLARISSA, WE HAVE A SLIGHT PROBLEM.

IS SHE PSYCHIC ...?

LEMME GUESS. SHE'S RIGHT ON THE MONEY?

I TAKE IT THEY WANT TO CONFIRM WHETHER OR NOT NISHIDA-KUN WAS AN EMPLOYEE HERE?

!!

NISHIDA-KUN'S WORK HISTORY SHOULD HAVE BEEN HIDDEN.

THEY'RE AWFULLY GOOD AT THEIR JOBS.

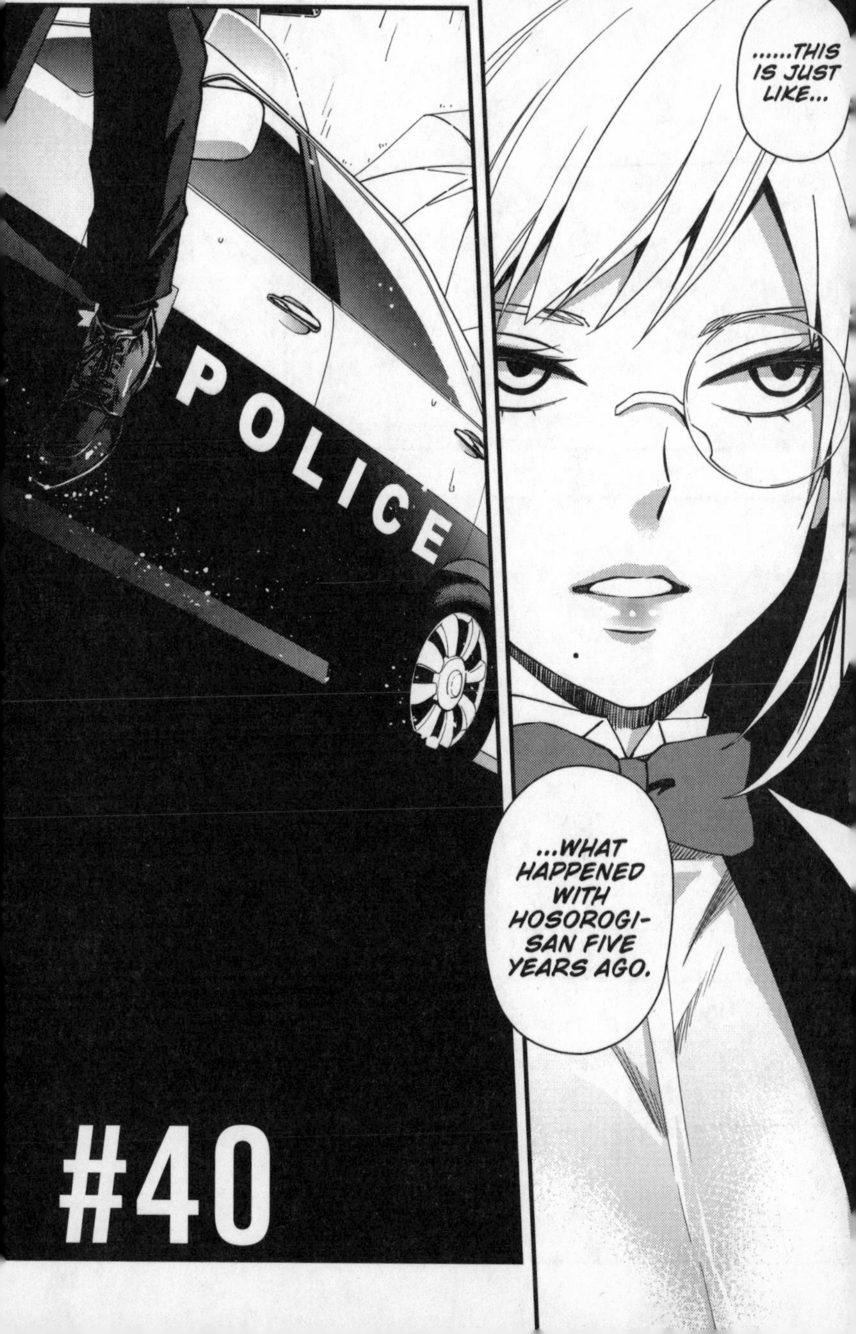
......THIS IS JUST LIKE...
...WHAT HAPPENED WITH HOSOROGI-SAN FIVE YEARS AGO.
POLICE
#40

BUT WHAT AM I SUPPOSED TO SAY TO THAT FAKE POLKA? AND HOW...?

AN HONEST... HEART-TO-HEART...?

YOUR FAMILY MEMBERS ARE ASSASSINS?

AND IF MISS SAYO WERE TO FIND OUT MY TRUE IDENTITY AS WELL......

DOES THAT HAVE ANYTHING TO DO WITH SHARKS?

...HM?

EITHER WAY, I THINK I'VE AVOIDED FAKE POLKA FOR AS LONG AS I CAN...

...ACTUALLY, I DOUBT SHE'D REALLY MIND.

122

THE POLICE... DID THEY COME TO ASK MORE QUESTIONS?

IF THIS IS ABOUT SOLITAIRE, I'M INVOLVED, SO THIS COULD BE BAD FOR ME...

SO WE'RE GOING TO PRESS THEM ABOUT THE SOLITAIRE CASE.

ALL RIGHT...

IF TAKUMI KURUYA'S INSIDE, THIS SHOULD GO QUICKLY...

DON'T GET TOO EXCITED, NOW.

AND I'VE GOT A GOOD FEELING HE IS.

EXCUSE US—COMING THROUGH.

WHOA!

I HAVEN'T SEEN YOUR FACES AROUND HERE BEFORE.

...WHO'RE YOU?

HOLD ON A SEC!

YOU DON'T LOOK MUCH LIKE A MANAGER...

...SO THIS IS YOUR TURF?

WELL, I'M SORT OF UNDERCOVER.

...YOU ARE?

AND...

I'M ALSO ONE OF THE OFFICERS IN CHARGE OF THE SOLITAIRE INVESTIGATION.

I MUST ASK YOU TO LEAVE.

NO CAN DO.

WE'RE WORKING A CASE UNDER THE CENTRAL OFFICE'S JURISDIC- TION.

OUR ORDERS ARE FROM THE *TOP*.

...THE SOLITAIRE CASE HAS NOTHING TO DO WITH THIS.

?

WE GOT A LEAD THAT A SUSPECTED MUGGER IS HIDING IN THIS BUILDING.

!?

...I'M IKEUCHI FROM THE MPD'S INVESTIGATIONS UNIT 1.

UNIT 1? WHAT'RE YOU DOING HERE...?

THE GUY RESPONSIBLE WORKS AT A BAR AROUND HERE.

IT HAPPENED LAST NIGHT. A REAL UGLY MUGGING IN THE STREET.

THAT'S CLARISSA'S BAR!

......!

IT'S CALLED "YOUTOU-KOROU."

I TRUST YOUR COMMUNITY SAFETY DIVISION'S HEARD OF IT?

WOULD ONE OF CLARISSA'S BOYS REALLY PULL A STUNT AT A TIME LIKE THIS?

STUFF INVOLVING OUR TROUBLE-MAKERS.

I DON'T THINK IT HAS ANYTHING TO DO WITH YOUR CASE.

WHAT?

YEAH, THERE'S BEEN SOME STUFF HAPPENING LATELY.

SURE. I'LL KEEP WATCH HERE.

...GUESS I'LL JUST HAVE TO WAIT AND SEE WHAT UNFOLDS.

I UNDERSTAND THE GRAVITY OF THE SOLITAIRE CASE, BUT I'D APPRECIATE YOU LETTING US TAKE THE LEAD HERE.

I SEE...

OH...AND IF YOU HAVE ANY TROUBLE WITH THE FORTUNE-TELLER IN THIS BUILDING, LET ME KNOW.

HE'S...

...AN ACQUAINTANCE OF MINE.

OHHH.

IT'S STARTED.

WHY...

WHAT IS IT, HIGURO-SAN?

NOTHING... I MEAN, I KNEW IT'D BE THE SHINJUKU BRANCH, BUT......

...IS HE HERE...?

IT'S THE DETECTIVE WHO DESTROYED THAT ORGANIZATION I TOLD YOU ABOUT YESTERDAY.

OH. YOU KNOW ONE OF THEM?

YOU'RE NOT WRONG.

...NO WAY WE CAN GO ABOUT THIS SAFELY WITH ONLY THE INFORMATION THAT CAME DOWN FROM ABOVE.

...MAYBE I OUGHT TO FIND OUT WHATEVER I CAN MYSELF.

I PERSONALLY ENJOY WHEN THAT HAPPENS.

AND AGAKURA FAILED SEVERAL TIMES DUE TO NOT HAVING ENOUGH INFO, RIGHT?

...BACK IN THE DAY, ONE OF OUR GUYS WAS A REALLY CAPABLE INFORMANT.

YOU GOT A CONTACT?

...HE'S WITH A *BUSINESS RIVAL IN SHINJUKU.*

BUT NOW...

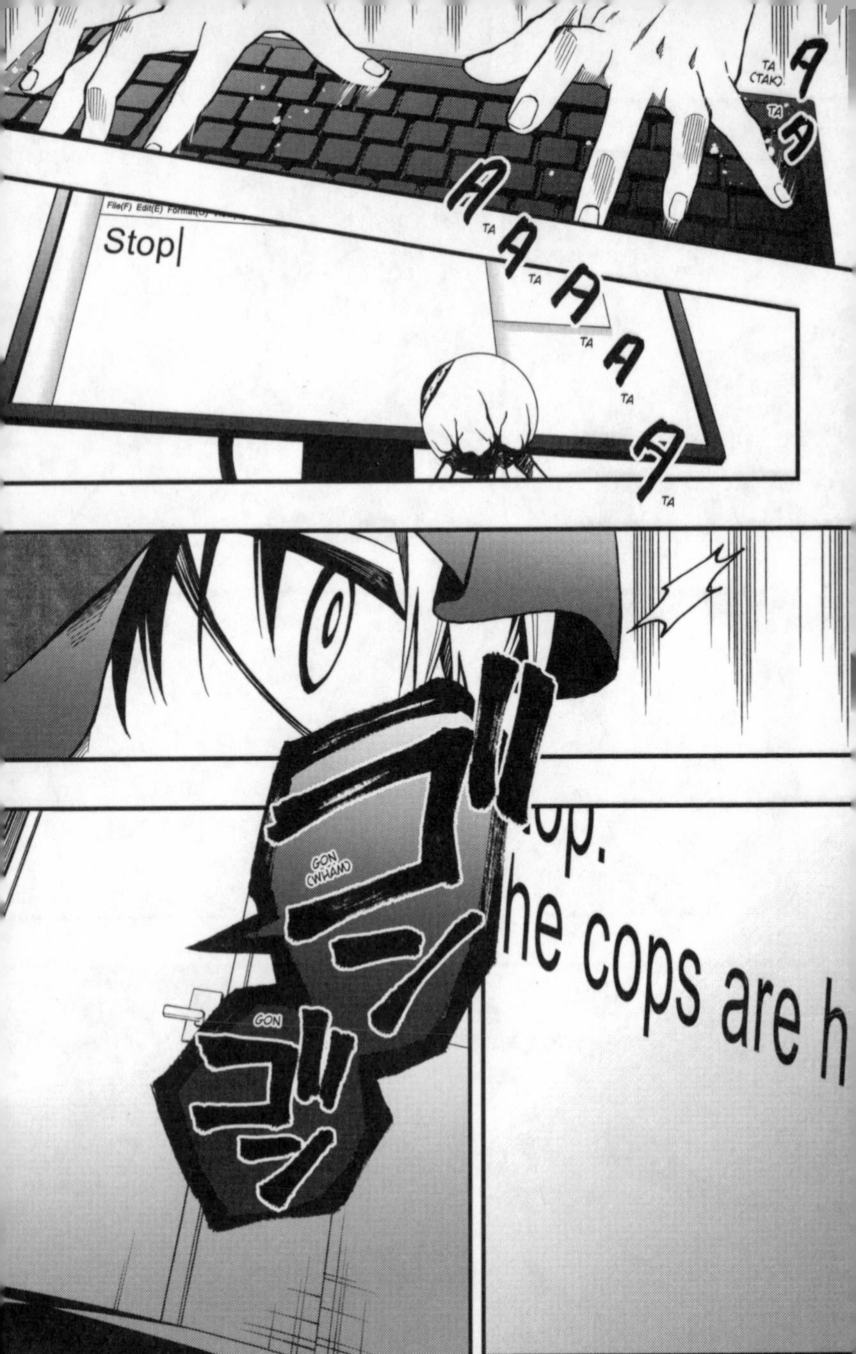

TA (TAK)
TA
TA
TA
TA
TA
TA
File(F) Edit(E) Format(O)
Stop|
GON (WHAM)
GON
op.
he cops are h

COMIIING.

HUH? WHAT? WHAT THE...?

WHO'S IN CHARGE HERE?

...I'M WITH THE POLICE.

IF YOU COULD, PLEASE EVACUATE THE PREMISES.

WE'RE LAUNCHING A FULL INVESTIGATION OF THIS BUILDING.

WHAT? ...IS HE DOING A HOME SEARCH?

......IF YOU MEAN WHO'S IN CHARGE OF THIS FORTUNE-TELLING BUSINESS, THAT'S ME.

THIS MAN IS SUSPECTED OF A MUGGING.

DO YOU REC-OGNIZE THIS FACE?

HUH?

ME- EE- EE- EE?

H- H- H-

...NO.

......

A MUGGING!? HERE!?

...WE RECEIVED INFORMATION THAT HE RAN INTO THIS BUILDING TO SEEK REFUGE, SO WE'D APPRECIATE YOUR COOPERATION WITH OUR INVESTIGATION.

N-NO! I DIDN'T DO IT-IT-IT-!!

VERY WELL.

Notepad
File(F) Edit(E) Format(O) View(V) Help(H)

Sorry, I screwed up.
Just do whatever
they say|

じっ
JI
(STARE)

SHOOT! I WASN'T ABLE TO TELL HIM BEFORE THEY GOT IN.

UH, COULD YOU SHOW ME THE PHOTO OF THAT MUGGER TOO?

SUSUSU
(SHUFFLE)
すすす

I WANT TO LOOK INTO THE IDENTITY OF THE MUGGER...

うず
UZU
(FIDGET)

うず
UZU
UZU
うず

A MUGGING? AT THIS TIME OF DAY? AND THE MUGGER RAN INTO THE VERY SAME BUILDING SOLITAIRE APPEARED ON? IS THERE SOME CONNECTION?

YES!

HUH!? WAIT...

...ARE YOU AFFILIATED WITH THIS BUSINESS?

Polka.
Polka.

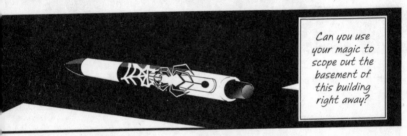

Can you use your magic to scope out the basement of this building right away?

I've got a bad feeling.

THE BASE-MENT...? WHY?

...feels familiar.

This whole thing...

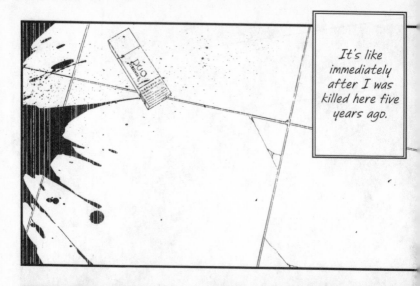

It's like immediately after I was killed here five years ago.

...I FOUND IT ALREADY.

If my hunch is correct, there's something down in the basement.

IN THE BASE-MENT...

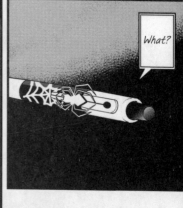

What?

IT'S THE CORPSE OF THAT MAN NAMED NISHIDA.

IT'S A CORPSE.

HEH HA HA!

A BODY.

HE'S DEAD.

DEAD.

AH HA HA!

......

You...

...I CAN BID MY PEACE AND QUIET FAREWELL.

THIS IS BAD... IF THEY FIND THAT IN THE BASEMENT...

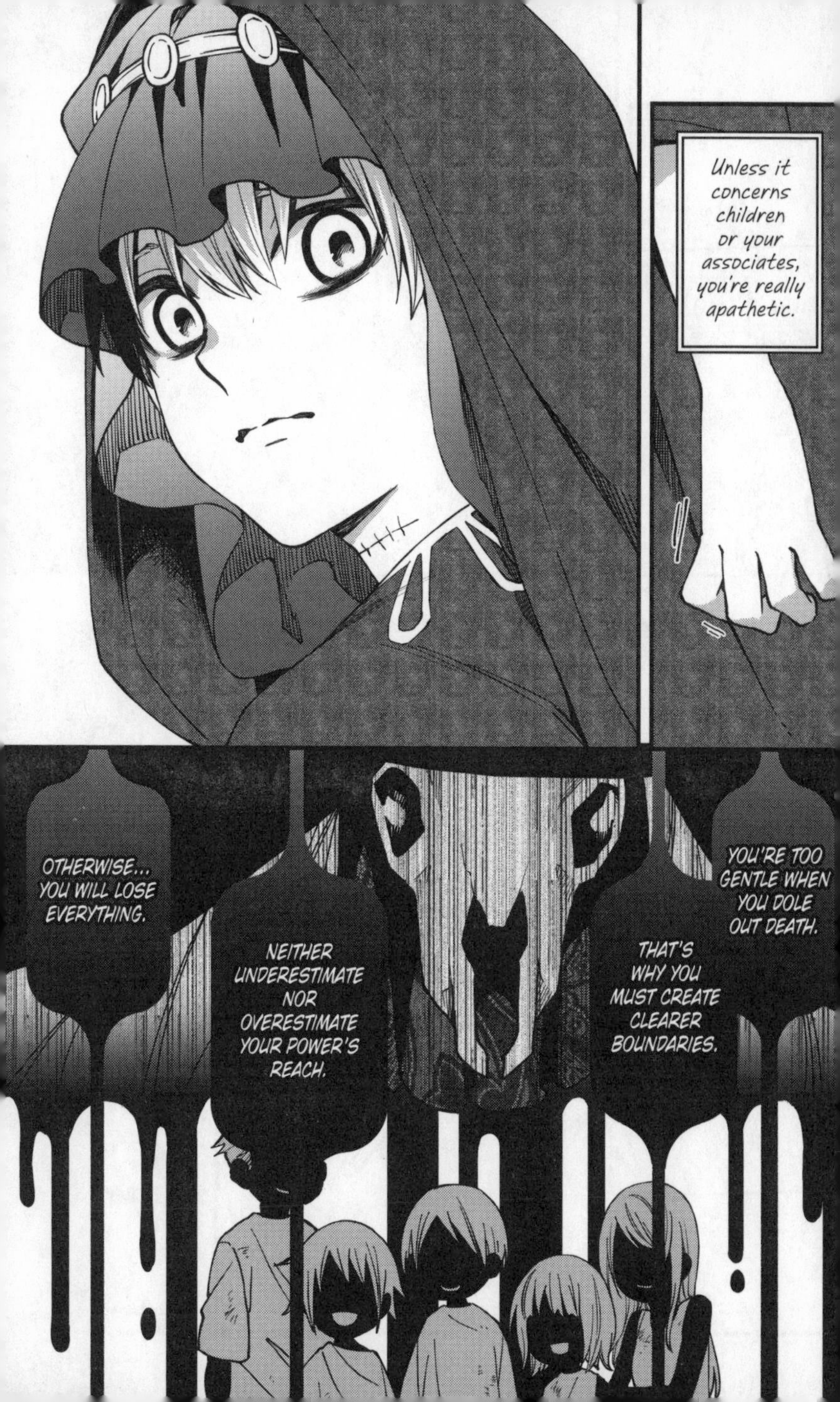

Unless it concerns children or your associates, you're really apathetic.
YOU'RE TOO GENTLE WHEN YOU DOLE OUT DEATH.
THAT'S WHY YOU MUST CREATE CLEARER BOUNDARIES.
NEITHER UNDERESTIMATE NOR OVERESTIMATE YOUR POWER'S REACH.
OTHERWISE... YOU WILL LOSE EVERYTHING.

BUT...

I WON'T DENY IT.

YES...

BE-LIEVE ME-EE!

COME ON-NN...

BE-LIEVE-EVE-EVE...

ME-E...

NO-

-O!

IT-T-T WASN'T ME-EE-EE!

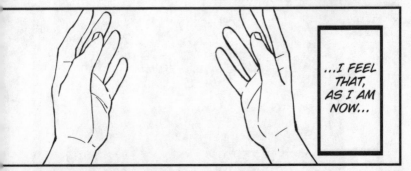

...I FEEL THAT, AS I AM NOW...

...MY HANDS WILL "REACH" FURTHER STILL.

GACHA
(KCHAK)

DEAD MOUNT
DEATH PLAY

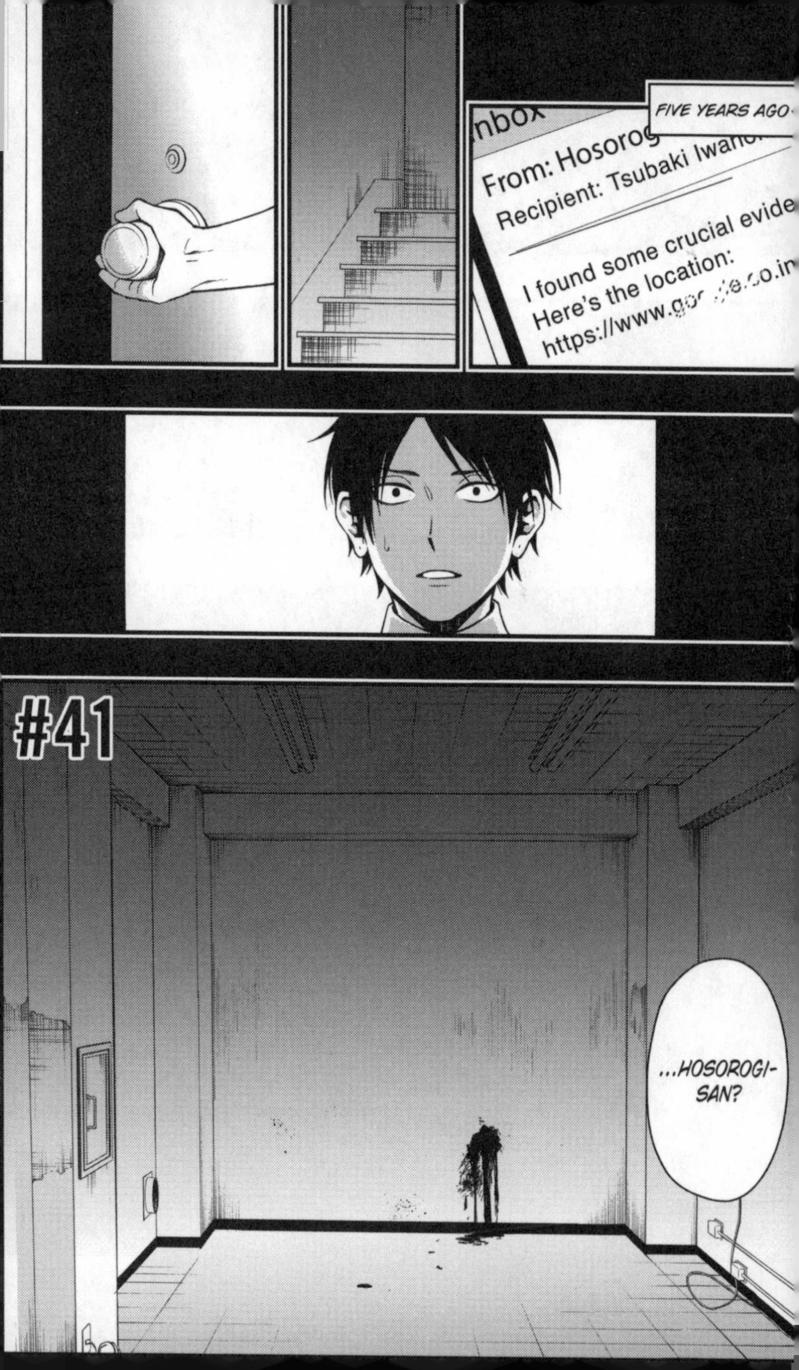
FIVE YEARS AGO
Inbox
From: Hosorog
Recipient: Tsubaki Iwano
I found some crucial evide
Here's the location:
https://www.go
#41
...HOSOROGI-SAN?

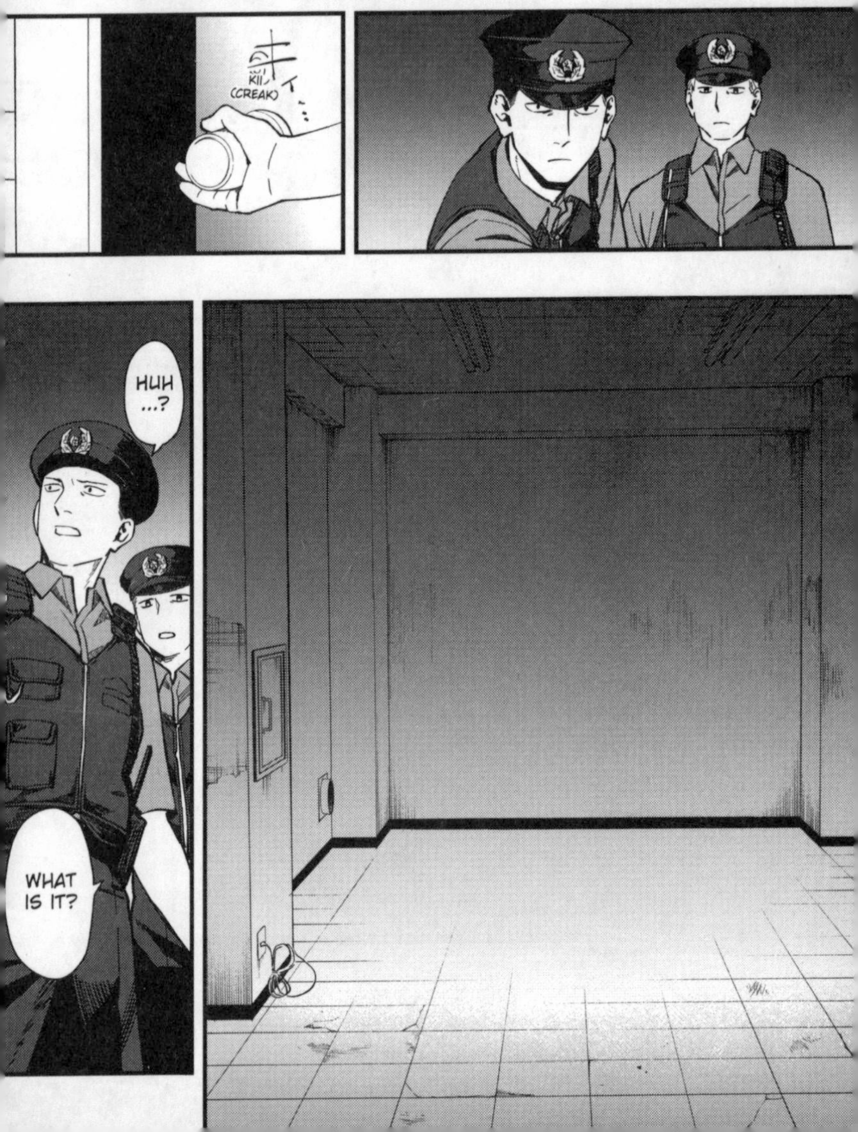
KII (CREAK)
HUH ...?
WHAT IS IT?

Y-YEAH. IT DOES.

HUH. YEAH, LOOKS LIKE AN EMPTY ROOM.

THERE'S *NOTHING*.

...DOESN'T LOOK LIKE ANYBODY'S HERE.

WE'RE CORPSES...

DON'T MAKE ANY NOISE...

DON'T MOVE... DON'T MOVE...

SO THE MAIN SAKURADAMON BRANCH HAS STARTED MAKING MOVES.

......

THE SHINJUKU MARKET WILL BE A WRECK...

LOOKS LIKE...

...THE MARKET PRICE FOR ASSASSINS WILL BE ON THE RISE.

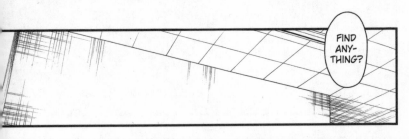

FIND ANY-THING?

HM? WHAT IS IT?

HUH?

I SEE.

...

NO, SIR. HE WASN'T DOWN THERE.

IF HE'S NOT IN THIS BUILDING, WE'LL CHECK THE NEIGHBORHOOD SURVEILLANCE CAMERAS.

IT'S ALSO POSSIBLE HE'S ALREADY FLED.

Y-YES, SIR.

UH, NOTH-ING...

IT'S JUST, IF HE'S NOT DOWN THERE, MAYBE HE'S UP ABOVE...

AT THE BUILDING WHERE POLKA'S STAY-ING?

THE POLICE?

WHERE ARE POLKA AND HIS FRIENDS?

...?

Yeah.

They're not local detectives. They're probably from the central office.

OUTSIDE, WAITING FOR THE POLICE TO WRAP UP.

IT'S A GOOD THING THE RAIN STOPPED.

SHARKS ...?

I'M FRIGHT-ENED, DARLING.

I KNOW.

I DISCOVERED IT WHILE I WAS SEARCHING THE BUILDING THAT NIGHT.

THERE ARE NO LIVING DOGS AROUND HERE.

A secret passage below the basement floor...?

......

I DID FIGURE OUT ONE THING, THOUGH.

...SINCE IT DIDN'T APPEAR TO HAVE BEEN USED FOR A WHILE, I DIDN'T GIVE IT ANY THOUGHT.

SECRET PASSAGES WERE PRETTY COMMON IN THE EMPIRE.

IT LOOKS TO BE CONNECTED TO ANOTHER BUILDING SOMEWHERE, BUT...

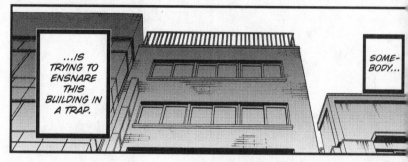

...IS TRYING TO ENSNARE THIS BUILDING IN A TRAP.

SOMEBODY...

The building's owner...

... Clarissa.

THEIR OBJECTIVE IS EITHER US...

...OR...

TAKUMI KURUYA.

YEP.

LOOKS LIKE HE WAS IN THERE AFTER ALL.

...THERE'S KOCHOU-CHAN.

わく WAKU

WAKU (GIDDY)

わく

I GUESS YESTERDAY WASN'T A ONE-TIME THING.

...I'D LOVE NOTHING MORE, BUT...

YOU SURE WE SHOULDN'T GO TOO?

SINCE THEY CAME RIGHT OUT WITHOUT A FIGHT, MAYBE WE SHOULD HANG BACK AND WATCH THEM FOR NOW...

...SHE SEEMS TO BE DOING A STORY ON POLKA SHINO-YAMA...

SHE'S A REPORTER WITH *WEEKLY DRY* NOW, RIGHT?

HUH? ISN'T HE FROM OUR SHINJUKU BRANCH OFFICE...?

THOSE UNIFORMED OFFICERS... WHO CAME ALONG WITH THE GUY FROM THE CENTRAL OFFICE...

AND TO SUGGEST ONE OF CLARISSA'S BARTENDERS WOULD FLEE INTO CLARISSA'S OWN BUILDING... DOESN'T MAKE SENSE.

THIS WHOLE STORY ABOUT THE CENTRAL OFFICE COMING HERE ON A MUGGING CASE SMELLS FISHY TO ME......

MAKES ME WONDER WHO TIPPED THEM OFF.

I WOULDN'T EVEN BE SURPRISED TO FIND OUT IT WAS SOLITAIRE'S DOING, BUT...

TON (TAP)
TON

THE TIMING'S JUST TOO GOOD.

YOU SAYING IT WAS FAKE INFORMATION?

...AS FIVE YEARS AGO.

IT'S THE SAME...

box

From: Hosorogi

Recipient: Tsub

I found some c

Here's the loca

https://www.go

...HOSOROGI-SAN HAD BEEN MISSING FOR SOME TIME WHEN I GOT AN EMAIL FROM HIM SAYING, "I FOUND SOME CRUCIAL EVIDENCE HERE."

BACK THEN...

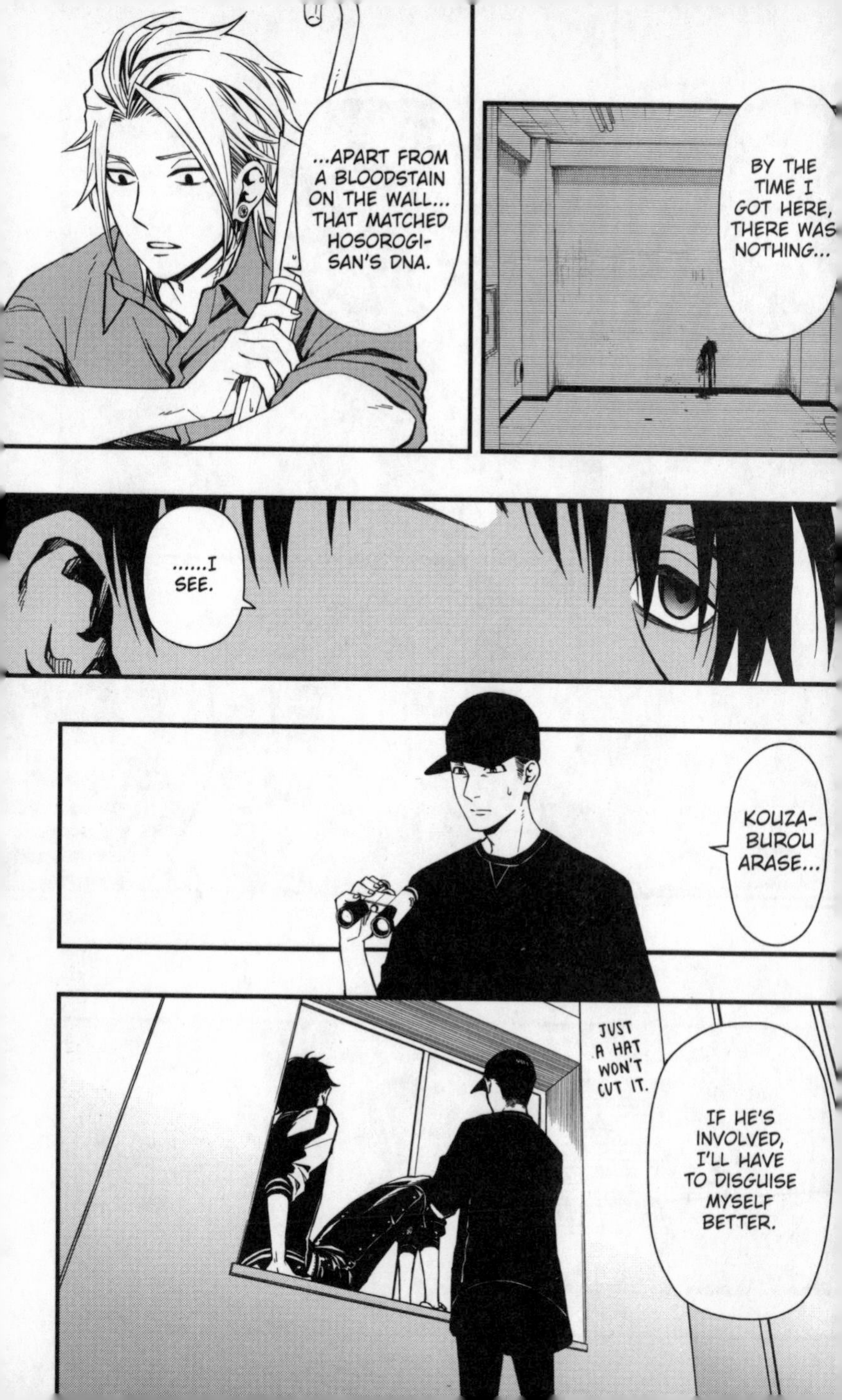
BY THE TIME I GOT HERE, THERE WAS NOTHING...
...APART FROM A BLOODSTAIN ON THE WALL... THAT MATCHED HOSOROGI-SAN'S DNA.
......I SEE.
KOUZA-BUROU ARASE...
IF HE'S INVOLVED, I'LL HAVE TO DISGUISE MYSELF BETTER.
JUST A HAT WON'T CUT IT.

......MOMOYA-SAN? WHAT IS IT?

HE MADE IT ALL THE WAY TO THE MAIN BASE OF SONS OF THE STYX ON HIS OWN...

...AND BEAT EIGHT OF THE BEST MEMBERS OF OUR FIGHTING UNIT WITHIN AN INCH OF THEIR LIVES.

...AS DESTINY.

THERE'S SUCH A THING...

ARE THE COPS WHO CAME LAST TIME NOT THE SAME ONES HERE TODAY?

WHAT ON EARTH IS GOING ON...?

I'LL WAIT AND WATCH A LITTLE LONGER...

WHAT...

...ARE YOU DOING HERE?

TAIPEI.

......

YOU DON'T HAVE TO REMIND ME. I'LL GO BACK.

YES.

YOUR JOB IS TO GUARD THE YOUNG LADY OF THE HOUSE, REMEMBER?

YOU LOST YOUR ARMS, LOST YOUR LEGS...

...AND STILL, YOU GOT BY WITHOUT BEING MADE A T'ING-FU.

...APART FROM CARRYING OUT YOUR DUTY TO PROTECT HER TO YOUR DEATH.

YOU HAVE NO FURTHER VALUE TO THE LEI FAMILY...

YOU NEEDN'T LORD YOURSELF OVER ME AS MY SUPERIOR, LIKE YOU DID IN THE OLD DAYS.

GYU (GRIP)

ぎゅ…

YOU DON'T HAVE TO TELL ME.

THE LEI FAMILY IS NO LONGER OF CONCERN TO ME.

ぽん

PON (PAT)

OH, NO?

I THINK YOU NEED TO LEARN HOW TO CONTROL THAT MOUTH OF YOURS.

ミシ

MISHI (GRIND)

IF YOU HAVE NO FURTHER CONNECTION TO THE FAMILY, THEN YOU'RE PART OF THE LOWLY RABBLE NOW.

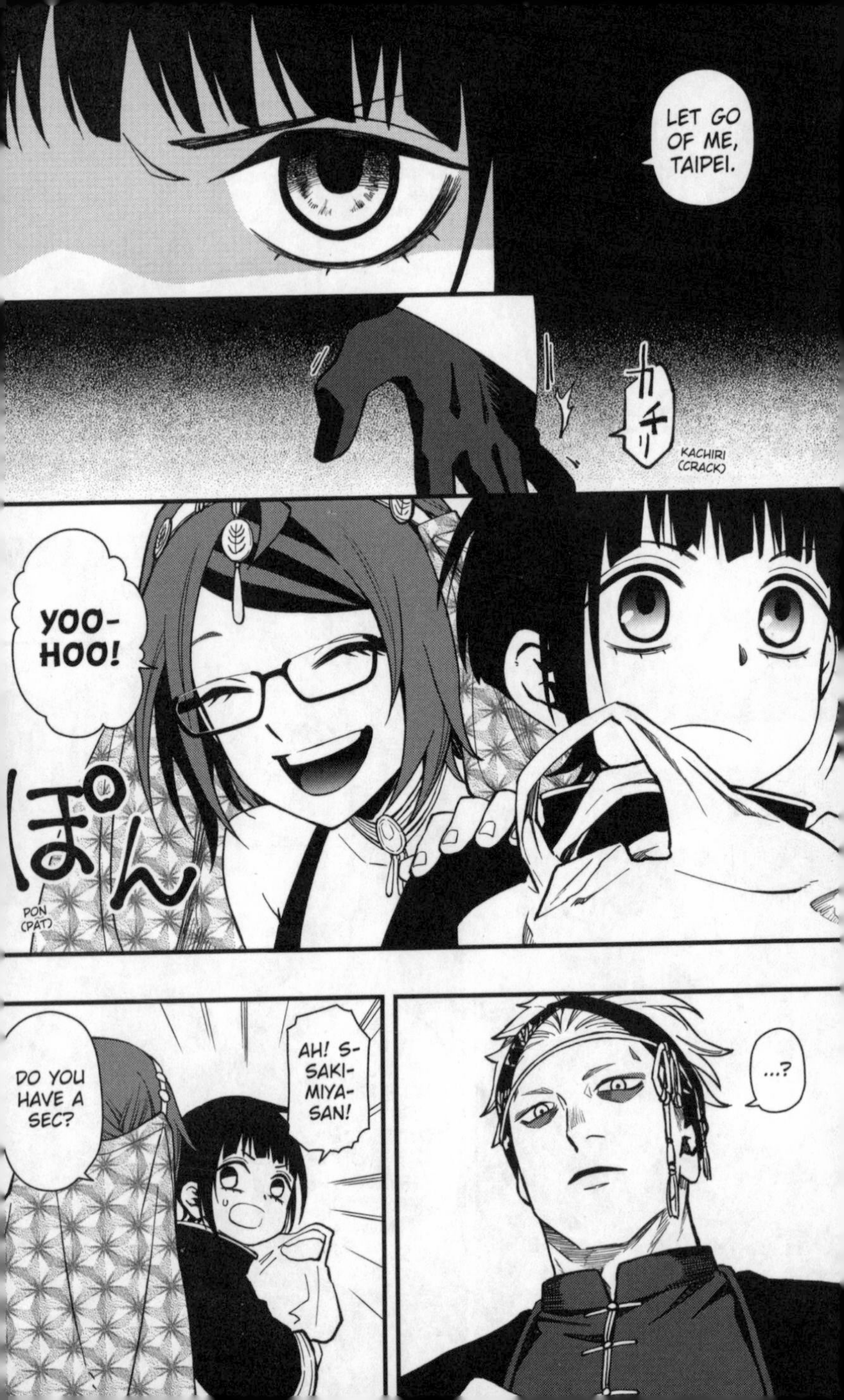
LET GO OF ME, TAIPEI.
カチリ
KACHIRI (CRACK)
YOO-HOO!
ぽん
PON (PAT)
...?
AH! S-SAKI-MIYA-SAN!
DO YOU HAVE A SEC?

UH.

スタタ (SCAMPER)

UM...

THINGS ARE A BIT OF A MESS AT THE BUILDING RIGHT NOW.

OH, UH, NO, THAT'S OKAY—

AH! ARE THESE GROCERIES? I'LL CARRY THEM FOR YOU!

WHO IS THAT GIRL...?

SHE'S NO AMATEUR.

NO WAY. IT COULDN'T BE YOUR FAMILY...

SHE'S PROBABLY KILLED...AT LEAST TEN PEOPLE.

EVEN AFTER FIVE YEARS, IT LOOKS LIKE KURAKI-SAN'S STILL ON HER GUARD.

...I SEE.

...ONE OF SHINJUKU'S ASSASSINS.

THAT GIRL IS PROBABLY...

I CAN'T BELIEVE HE'S HERE, OF ALL PLACES.

...TAKUMI KURUYA.

AND...

THE SON OF THE SHINOYAMA FAMILY...... POLKA...

...ACCOMPANIED BY AN ASSASSIN AND AN INFORMANT... HUH?

SURU (SSK)

I WAS AFRAID THIS WOULD BE A BORING JOB, BUT I'M GLAD I WAS WRONG.

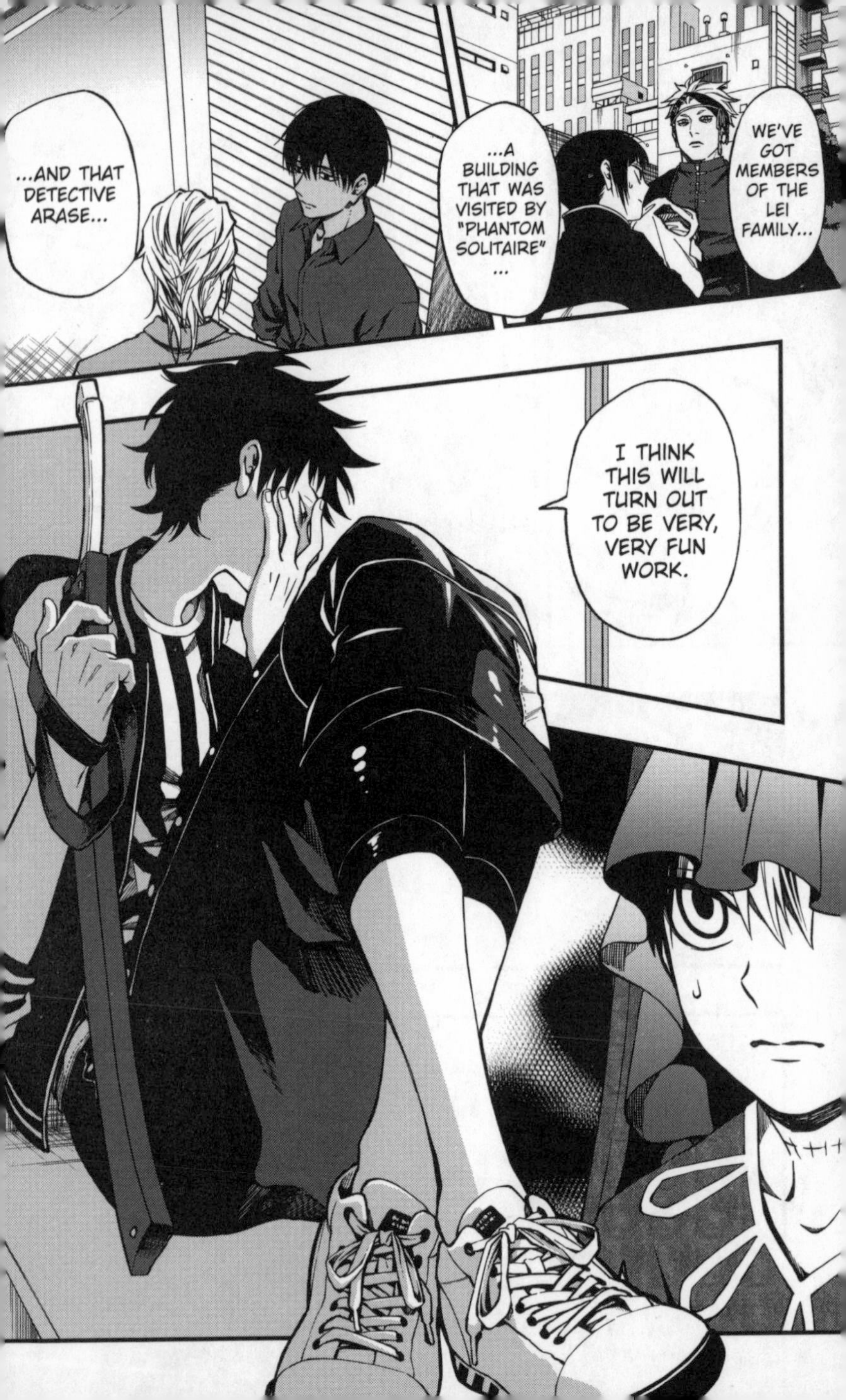
WE'VE GOT MEMBERS OF THE LEI FAMILY...
...A BUILDING THAT WAS VISITED BY "PHANTOM SOLITAIRE"...
...AND THAT DETECTIVE ARASE...
I THINK THIS WILL TURN OUT TO BE VERY, VERY FUN WORK.

PIRORIN
(DING)

I'LL HOLD ALL THAT, SO PLEASE...

AH. UM.

BRAVO!

......

To my beloved little brother, Please don't say such cold things. No matter what Father and that overgrown jerk say, I, at least, will always looooove you, Xiaoyu. You mean more to me than anything. As proof, I wiped out that cocky Taipei's savings account and transferred all his funds into your account, Xiaoyu. So never forget your older sister's here for you.
Your one and only knight in shining armor, Imbi

HM? OH, SHE WAS HERE JUST A MINUTE AGO.

......HUH? WHERE'D SAKIMIYA-SAN GO...?

NEW SHARK MERCH!

SHE HAS A WAY OF DISAPPEARING INTO THIN AIR...

......IT'S THAT GIRL FROM BEFORE...

...CAN I HELP YOU?

I'M ON THE SHINOYAMA FAMILY'S SIDE.

DON'T WORRY.

...
SHE'S NO AMATEUR.

I CAN TELL BY HOW SHE WALKS AND MANEUVERS HERSELF...

"AN ALLY OF THE SHINO-YAMAS"...

...DOESN'T MEAN "AN ALLY OF POLKA-KUN," NOW, DOES IT?

NIKO (GRIN)

SO SHE'S PART OF POLKA SHINO-YAMA'S CREW...

IT'S SHIN-JUKU.

THIS ISN'T THE SHINO-YAMAS' TURF.

AND IT'S PACKED WITH ALL SORTS OF PEOPLE.

SO YOU'D BETTER TAKE CARE, YOU HEAR?

THIS WEAK AURA OF LIFE SHE HAS...

WHAT IS THIS?

...SHE'S NOT LIKE ANY PERSON I'VE EVER SEEN BEFORE.

...I SEE.

SO IT REALLY IS A DEN OF THIEVES.

THE REPORTER'S GONE HOME TOO.

...THEY'RE LEAVING...?

I DON'T BLAME HER. TODAY WASN'T A GOOD DAY FOR AN INTERVIEW...

#42

I BET YOU'RE SUPER-PUMPED FOR TOMORROW, EH, CHIEF!?

UUUH... YEAH, I GUESS.

THERE'S A BIG CONSPIRACY BEHIND ALL THIS! I CAN SMELL IT!

I REALLY WONDER ABOUT THE KIND OF PERSON WHO'D USE HER OWN BOSS AS A GUINEA PIG.

SECOND FORTUNE-TELLING GUINEA PIG

IN THE END, YOU WEREN'T EVEN ABLE TO GET YOUR FORTUNE TOLD.

AH. SORRY FOR DRAGGING YOU OUT HERE FOR NOTHING TODAY.

I WANT YOU...

...TO DROP THIS CASE.

ANYWAY, LEAVING ALL THAT ASIDE...

KOCHOU.

168

YOU'VE ALLIED YOURSELF WITH BIG-SHOT POLITICIANS AND YAKUZA BOSSES, AND NOW YOU WANNA JUST WAIT AND SEE WITH THIS!?

WHY!?

WHA...!?

I JUST WANT YOU TO PULL OUT.

DON'T BE AN IDIOT. I'M NOT SAYING OUR MAGAZINE IS GOING TO PULL OUT FROM THIS STORY.

FIVE YEARS BACK, THE POLICE FOUND BLOODSTAINS MATCHING ONE OF THEIR HIGHER-UPS THERE.

THAT BUILDING *HAS A PAST*. FOR DECADES, IT'S BEEN AT THE CENTER OF ALL KINDS OF RUMORS.

AND NOW, THEY'RE LAUNCHING A MAJOR INVESTIGATION FOR A MUGGER WHO SOUGHT REFUGE IN IT? THAT'S NOT NORMAL.

HAND IT OVER TO HIMURA ATARI IN THE LOCAL NEWS SECTION. HE'S A VETERAN.

THIS IS NO JOB FOR A ROOKIE TO TAKE ON.

THIS IS MY STORY.

NO.

GU (CLENCH)

HERE'S PHOTOGRAPHIC EVIDENCE, CHIEF!

I EXPOSED THE TRUTH, CHIEF!

Major Politician Caught in Scandal

The Shocking Truth

I DID IT, CHIEF!

IF I FORCE HER OUT, I'LL HAVE A REPEAT OF LAST YEAR WHERE SHE WENT OUT AND COVERED A STORY ON HER OWN TIME ANYWAY.

BUT SHE'S TOO GOOD FOR ME TO JUST FIRE HER OVER IT.

AAAH...

170

STICK TO THE OCCULT ANGLE AS THE OCCULT REPORTER AND TELL THE "FORTUNE-TELLER CORPSE GOD" STORY.

!

...FINE. THEN WE'LL COMPROMISE.

DON'T INVESTIGATE ANYTHING BEYOND HIS FORTUNE-TELLING.

BUT DON'T TAKE IT ANY FURTHER THAN THAT.

!

BUT WHAT?

YOU DON'T TRUST YOUR HUNCH THAT POLKA SHINOYAMA IS AT THE HEART OF ALL THIS?

OKAY. BUT...

IN EXCHANGE, IF ANYTHING ELSE COMES UP, I'LL GIVE YOU FIRST DIBS ON EXCLUSIVE NEWS.

AND PULLING THAT FACE ISN'T GOING TO DO ANYTHING.

AWWW...

DON'T THINK SO LITTLE OF ME, CHIEF EDITOR!

ばっ

BA (WHIP)

HEH...

HEH HEH.

POLKA SHINOYAMA IS THE KEY PLAYER IN THIS CASE.

MY HUNCHES ARE NEVER WRONG.

I'LL MAKE HIM THE CENTER OF THIS CASE IF I HAVE TO!

OH YES.

GUE (CLENCH)

WHATEVER YOU DO, DON'T FORGE ANY EVIDENCE OR ANYTHING, OKAY?

HERE I GO!!

...WAIT. YOU...

I GOT THOSE THINGS YOU ASKED ME FOR......

UM...... MISS.

BUT WHAT ARE YOU GOING TO USE "THAT" FOR? AND SO MANY OF THEM...

YOU DON'T HAVE TO EXPLAIN THE SHARK MERCH.

IF AN AMATEUR MEDDLES WITH SAID MYSTERIES, HE'LL BE SWALLOWED WHOLE BY THE *GREAT DETECTIVE SHARKOLUMBO*, SO BE CAREFUL.

HEH-HEH. THAT'S A SECRET.

KOTSUN (POKE)
こつん

THERE ARE STILL MANY UNSOLVED MYSTERIES WHEN IT COMES TO SHARKS AND THE WORLD AT LARGE.

PEKO (BOW)

WELL, I'LL GO AND GET DINNER READY, THEN.

"SHARKOLUMBO"?

R- RIGHT...

SO WHAT'S IN THERE, REALLY?

GASA (RUSTLE)

MAGIC-STORING STONES

RAW GEMS!

OH! MAGIC-STORING STONES ...!

JUST SOMETHING TO COVER MY ROOM AND BOARD.

OH, NOTHING MUCH.

• STONES THAT HAVE MAGIC STORED IN THEM.

• KNOWN AS "JEWELS" IN THIS WORLD.

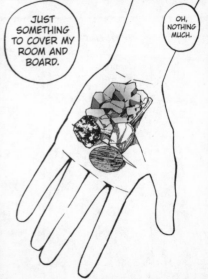

I CAN SEE HOW THAT'D BE CHEAPER THAN BUYING THEM FROM JEWELRY STORES...

I HAD XIAOYU-KUN GO AROUND TO THE ACCESSORY SHOPS AND GENERAL STORES TO BUY UP THEIR ENTIRE STOCKS FOR ME.

ARE YOU SURE I CAN HAVE THEM...?

IT'S FINE.

AFTER ALL, THE REAL POLKA WAS SAVED THANKS TO YOU.

DID SHE HEAR IT FROM THE MASTER?

SO SHE KNOWS THIS POLKA'S A FAKE TOO.........

!

ALSO... WHAT'S HE GOING TO USE ALL THOSE RAW GEMS FOR?

AND HE SAVED THE "REAL POLKA"... WHAT DOES THAT MEAN?

OH, SO YOUR END GOAL IS EXPENSIVE GEMS.

THE MORE TRANSPARENT, THE MORE EFFECTIVE, BUT......

YOU CAN USE THESE?

THANK YOU SO MUCH...!

WHAT'S HE NEED THOSE FOR?

KURU (KNEAD)
KURU
KURU
KURU
KURU

GEMS...

WELL... THERE'S ONE MAJOR THING I CAN THINK OF DOING......

SO? SO WHAT CAN YOU DO WITH ALL THESE?

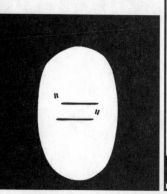

AND THAT'S...

IN FACT, I KNOW WHAT THE FIRST THING I'M GOING TO DO IS NOW THAT I HAVE THESE STONES IN HAND.

WHAT'S... GOING ON HERE...?

......?

A NUMBER OF STORES...

...HAVE BEEN PART OF A SMALL-SCALE BUYOUT OF RAW GEM-STONES...

!

I WONDER WHO DID IT AND WHAT THEY'RE STOCKING UP FOR.

SO... WHAT DO WE DO ABOUT OUR PROBLEM NOW?

とん
TON
(TAP)

FOR THE TIME BEING, LET'S JUST MAKE SURE IT'S NOT DISCOVERED.

I CONTACTED CLARISSA, BUT WHAT ABOUT THE CORPSE IN THE BASEMENT PASSAGE?

WHAT'S THIS ABOUT!?

!?

A CORPSE!?

ピタ
PITA
(FREEZE)

178

M-M-M-MAYBE-EE-EE-EE.

AM I GOING TO BE KILLED TOO!?

AAAH...

GATA (TRMBL)
GATA
GATA
GATA
GATA
GATA

I KNOW WE TOOK ADVANTAGE OF THE CONFUSION FROM THE INVESTIGATION TO SEND URAI BACK TO CLARISSA'S BAR, BUT...

CHANCES ARE TEN TO ONE THAT IT'S A BARTENDER NAMED NISHIDA WHO WORKED FOR CLARISSA.

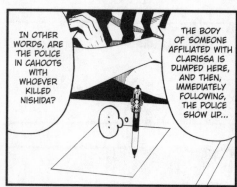

IN OTHER WORDS, ARE THE POLICE IN CAHOOTS WITH WHOEVER KILLED NISHIDA?

THE BODY OF SOMEONE AFFILIATED WITH CLARISSA IS DUMPED HERE, AND THEN, IMMEDIATELY FOLLOWING, THE POLICE SHOW UP...

WOOOW.

OH, SO HE WORKED AT CLARISSA'S PLACE...

...HM?

I'M GOING TO SLIP OUT THE BACK, SO TAKE CARE OF THE REST FOR ME!

WE'LL TALK MORE LATER!

BATA (SCAMPER)

BATA

UH-OH... IT'S ARASE.

SAAAA (PAAALE)

OH. OKAY.

SEE YA!

IF YOU NEED ANYTHING, CONTACT ME ON MY CELL.

......

KACHA (CLACK)

WOOOOW! THIS ALL LOOKS DELICIOUS!

KON (KNOCK)

KON

JUST DOING MY JOB...

I'VE ALWAYS THOUGHT SO, BUT YOU'RE A REALLY GOOD CHEF.

YOU'RE EATING? SORRY FOR INTER-RUPTING.

PEKO (BOW) ぺこ

AH... HELLO.

YO!

SO.

I'M JUST GOING TO ASK YOU POINT-BLANK.

ARE YOU GUYS LOOKING FOR THE MUGGER TOO?

KYORO (LOOK) キョロ

NO, UNFORTUNATELY, WE'RE STILL ON THE SOLITAIRE CASE.

WHY DID SOLITAIRE COME TO THIS BUILDING?

THE REASON SOLITAIRE CAME HERE...

YOU KNOW THE ANSWER TO THAT, DON'T YOU?

THIS POLICEMAN SHOULDN'T KNOW ANYTHING ABOUT THAT SYMBOL.

CHIRA (GLANCE)

...AH!?

HM?

NO... I HAVE NO IDEA WHY.

Polka. Polka!

p—

COME ON. THERE'S NO POINT HIDING THINGS FROM ME NOW.

The truth is—

What I wrote down for this detective before......

......!

......!?

......? I DON'T KNOW WHAT YOU'RE TALKING ABOUT.

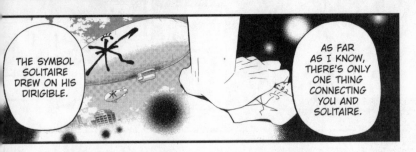

THE SYMBOL SOLITAIRE DREW ON HIS DIRIGIBLE.

AS FAR AS I KNOW, THERE'S ONLY ONE THING CONNECTING YOU AND SOLITAIRE.

SO TELL ME.

HOSOROGI-SAN'S THE ONLY ONE WHO KNOWS ABOUT THAT SYMBOL.

YOU'RE IN TOUCH WITH HOSOROGI-SAN SOMEHOW, AREN'T YOU?

IF POSSIBLE...

...CAN YOU LET ME SEE HIM?

......

HEY.

IF YOU DON'T BELIEVE IN ME...IF I CAN'T FORM A RELATIONSHIP OF MUTUAL TRUST WITH YOU, THEN THERE'S NOTHING I CAN SAY...

PUI (SNUB)

...SO IN OTHER WORDS, YOU DIDN'T BELIEVE MY "FORTUNE-TELLING" SKILLS FROM THE GET-GO.

WE'VE COME TOO FAR...

...FOR YOU TO WEASEL OUT OF THIS.

ピンポーン

PINPOOON (DING-DONG)

BUT FOR NOW, I HAVE TO ORGANIZE THAT INFOR-MATION......

...SHEESH. IT'S BEEN TOO MANY THINGS TODAY, ONE AFTER ANOTHER......

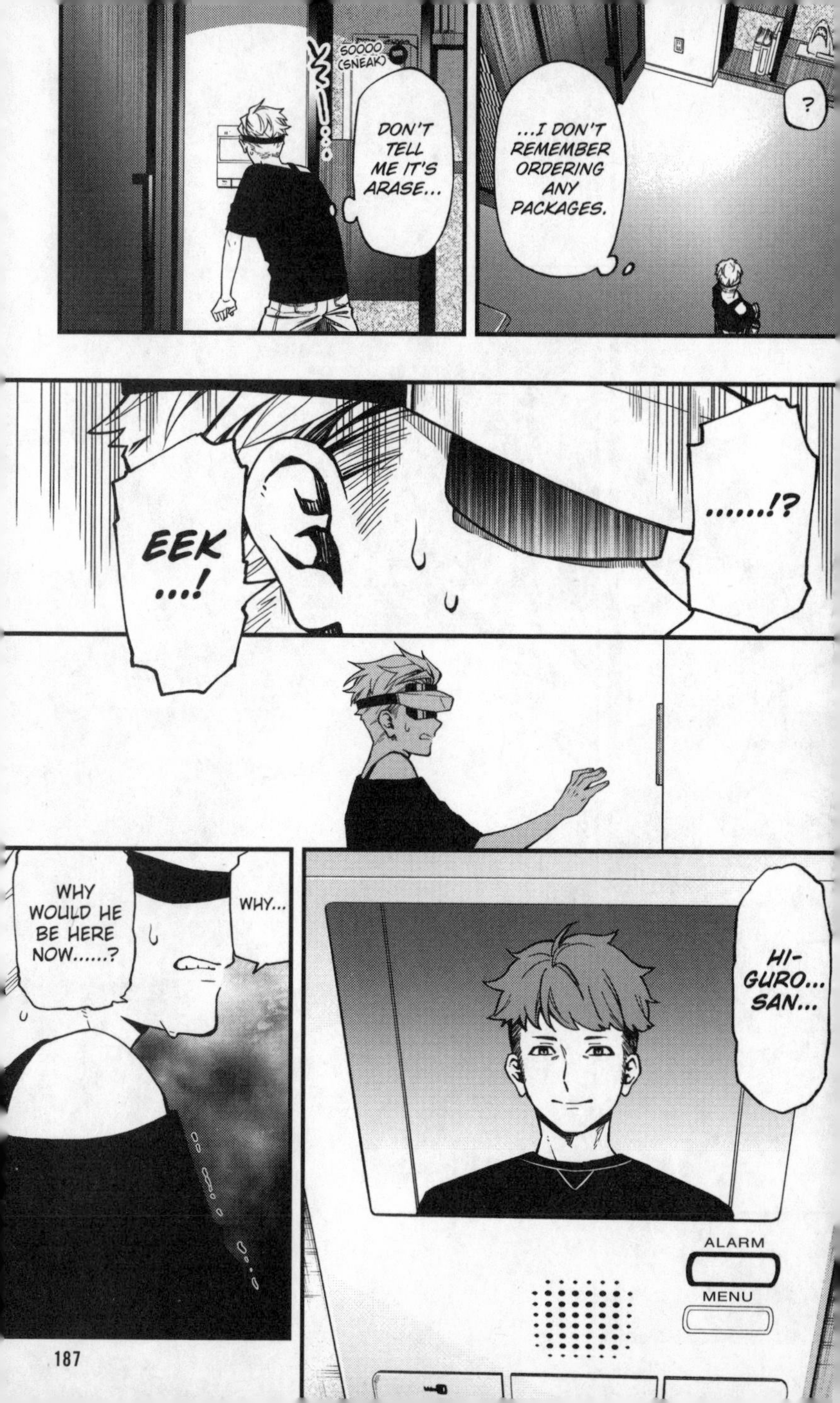
SOOOO (SNEAK)
DON'T TELL ME IT'S ARASE...
...I DON'T REMEMBER ORDERING ANY PACKAGES.
?
EEK ...!
......!?
WHY WOULD HE BE HERE NOW......?
WHY...
HI-GURO... SAN...
ALARM
MENU

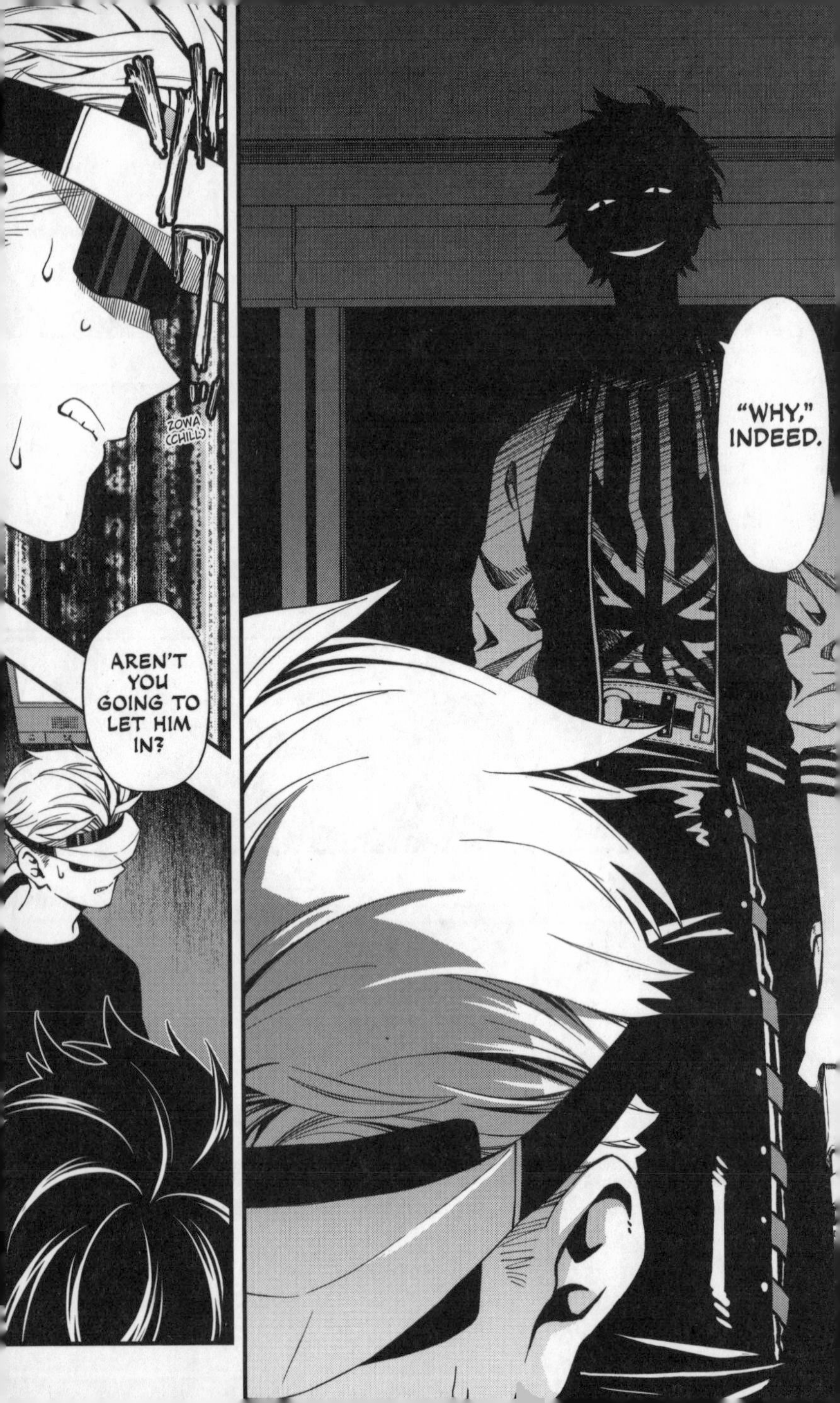
"WHY," INDEED.
ZOWA (CHILL)
AREN'T YOU GOING TO LET HIM IN?

HIGURO-SAN... IS A LONELY GUY, SO HE MIGHT CRY, YOU KNOW?

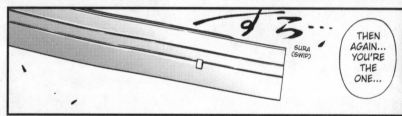

THEN AGAIN... YOU'RE THE ONE...

SURA
(SWIP)

...WHO MIGHT END UP IN TEARS, HMM?

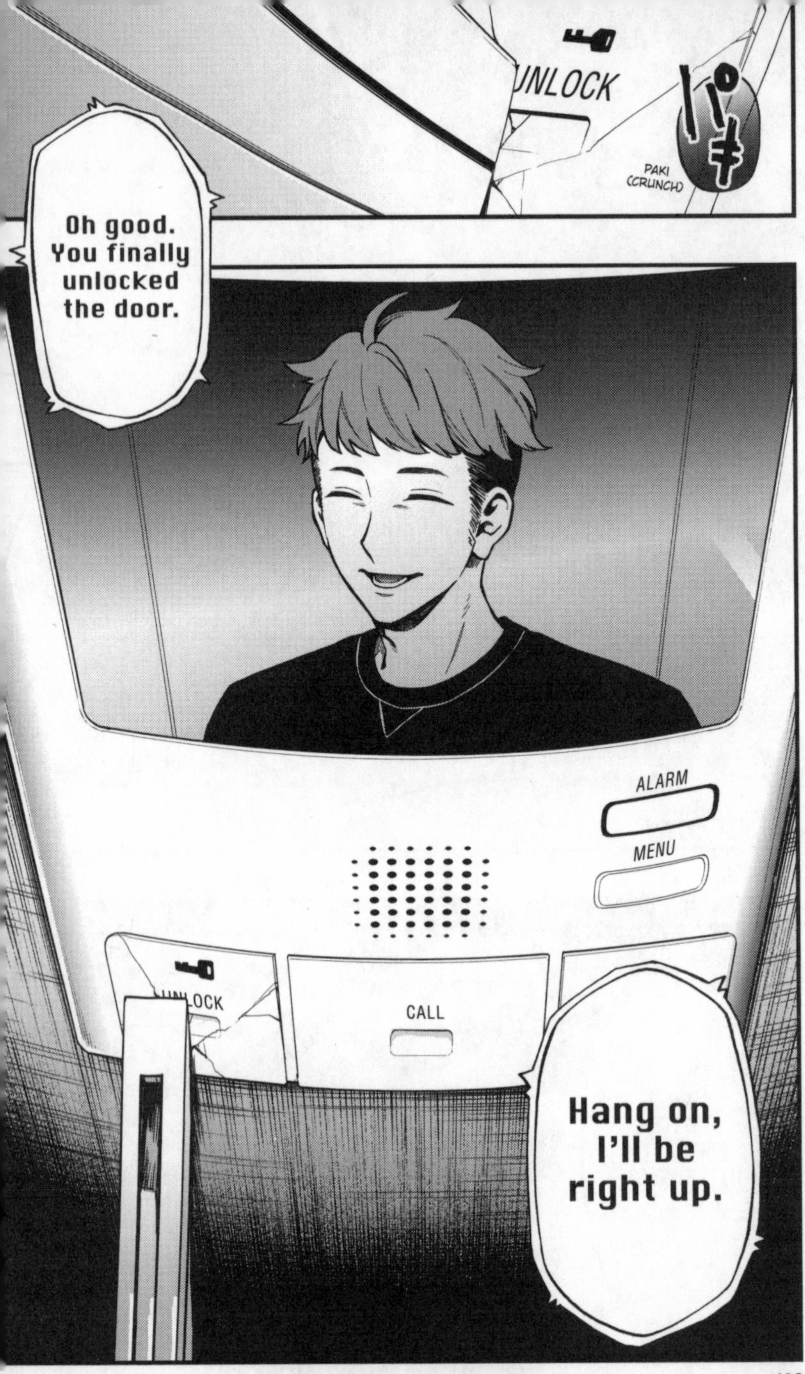
UNLOCK
パキ
PAKI (CRUNCH)
Oh good. You finally unlocked the door.
ALARM
MENU
UNLOCK
CALL
Hang on, I'll be right up.

#43

SLOWLY BUT SURELY...

...THEY REALIZE THAT DANGER IS DRAWING NEAR.

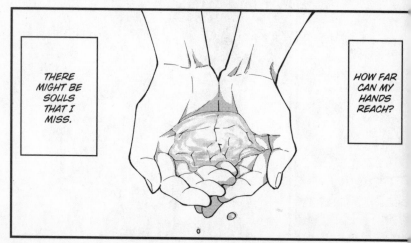

THAT'S PRECISELY WHY I MUST BE CAUTIOUS...

#43

CAN YOU...

FOOD...

...BOY?

HOW ABOUT YOU COME CLEAN WITH ME...

192

"IF YOU STILL BELIEVE IN ME, THEN KEEP PURSUING IT."

"YOUR ANSWER IS ON THE PIECE OF PAPER THAT GUIDED YOU EARLIER.

KA (TAK)

KA

...PROVE TO ME YOU'RE NOT INVOLVED WITH THE UNDERBELLY OF THE POLICE FORCE?

...SAYS THE PERSON WAITING FOR YOU.

I DUNNO... BUT EITHER WAY, HE'S RIGHT.

FOLLOWING UP ON THE INFORMATION ON THE PAPER I GOT DURING THAT FORTUNE-TELLING SESSION COMES FIRST.

...SO POLKA SHINOYAMA REALLY IS IN CONTACT WITH INSPECTOR HOSOROGI?

SINCE WE CAN'T TRUST THEM, IT LOOKS LIKE WE'RE STUCK.

YOU SAID IT.

...I'D LOVE TO...

...BUT IF WE'RE NOT CAREFUL, THEY COULD CATCH WIND OF OUR ACTIVITIES.

SO WE'RE NOT GOING TO ACT IMMEDIATELY?

I FULLY UNDERSTAND WHY HOSOROGI-SAN DISAPPEARED.

So trust nobody.
On the west side of the place indicated, there's one more garage.
There's a signpost.
The key is behind the first 383 mirror.

PO
(FLIP)

...DAMN IT.

PO

IT'S STARTING TO RAIN AGAIN.

NICE PLACE YOU GOT HERE.

HA HA.

YOU HATE MY GUTS, DON'T YOU?

...WHAT ARE YOU DOING HERE, AFTER ALL THIS TIME?

BUT, MAN, I HAVEN'T SEEN YOU IN FOREVER.

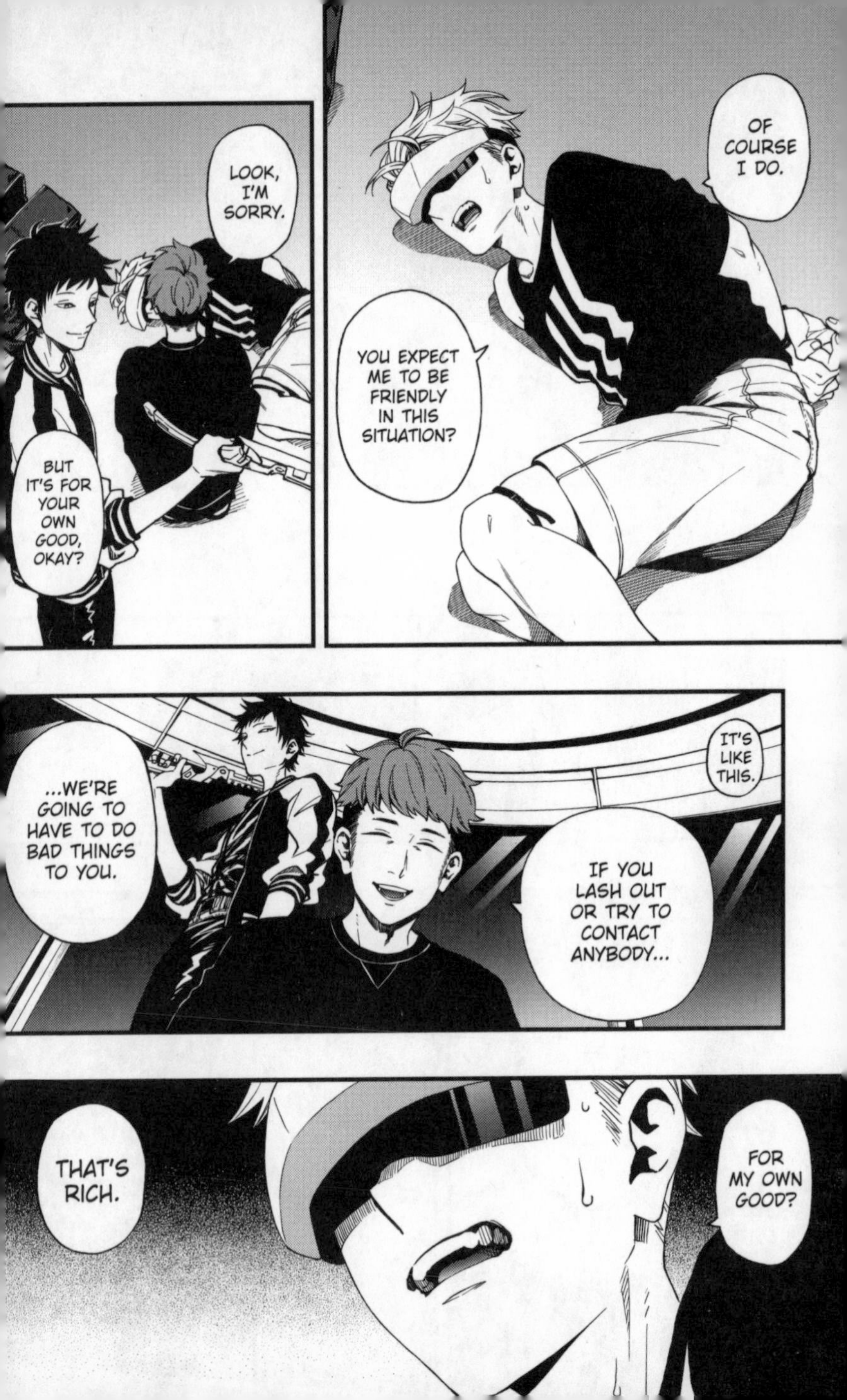
OF COURSE I DO.
YOU EXPECT ME TO BE FRIENDLY IN THIS SITUATION?
LOOK, I'M SORRY.
BUT IT'S FOR YOUR OWN GOOD, OKAY?
IT'S LIKE THIS.
IF YOU LASH OUT OR TRY TO CONTACT ANYBODY...
...WE'RE GOING TO HAVE TO DO BAD THINGS TO YOU.
FOR MY OWN GOOD?
THAT'S RICH.

BUT, LOOK, LET'S PIN THE BLAME ON ARASE AND PATCH THINGS UP BETWEEN US.

YEAH, THAT WAS A REAL SHAME.

WHEN ARASE WIPED OUT SONS OF THE STYX, YOU WENT ON THE LAM TO SAVE YOUR OWN SKIN.

YOU FIGURE IT OUT?

KURU

......

...YOU MUST AT LEAST KNOW THAT I'M WORKING FOR CLARISSA NOW.

SURE. THAT'S WHY I'M HERE.

KURU (TWIRL)

KURU

...THE ONE WHO MUGGED NISHIDA...

...WAS YOU?

YOU...

JUDGING BY YOUR REACTION JUST NOW...YOU HAD TO THINK FOR A MOMENT, DIDN'T YOU?

DO (STAB)

GNH!

YOU WONDERED, DIDN'T YOU?

WHETHER TO SAY "KILLED" OR "MUGGED."

YOU CHOSE YOUR WORDS.

TON (TAP)

トン

TON

トン

I FIGURED YOU KNEW...

...ABOUT THE DEAD BODY.

AAGH...

DOSU (STAB)

GUH ...!

.......!

SO IT REALLY WAS YOU...!

GIRI (GRIT)

GATA (TRMBL)

GATA

.......!

MAKES YOU FALL FOR LEADING QUESTIONS YOU WOULD NORMALLY NEVER FALL FOR.

PAIN IS GOOD.

IT DULLS A PERSON'S JUDGMENT.

NUCHA (SPLAK)

ALL THE MORE FOR SOMEONE WHO FEARS PAIN, LIKE YOU.

HFF...

HFF...

...DID YOU MANAGE TO HIDE THE BODY?

HOW...

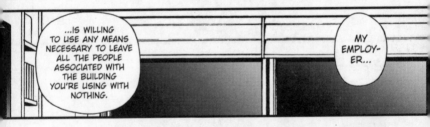

...IS WILLING TO USE ANY MEANS NECESSARY TO LEAVE ALL THE PEOPLE ASSOCIATED WITH THE BUILDING YOU'RE USING WITH NOTHING.

MY EMPLOY-ER...

ARE YOU SURE YOU SHOULD BE SAYING ALL THIS IN FRONT OF ME?

OR ELSE, WE CAN'T MAKE THEM ALL SUSPECTS.

SO WE NEED THE BODY FROM THE MUGGING TO BE FOUND IN THAT BUILDING.

NOW THAT YOU'VE HEARD IT, YOU'RE ALL OUT OF OPTIONS.

SURE.

YOU'RE SMART, SO YOU UNDERSTAND WHY, DON'T YOU?

...

HE MIGHT...

...STILL HAVE OPTIONS...

...HI-GURO-SAN.

?

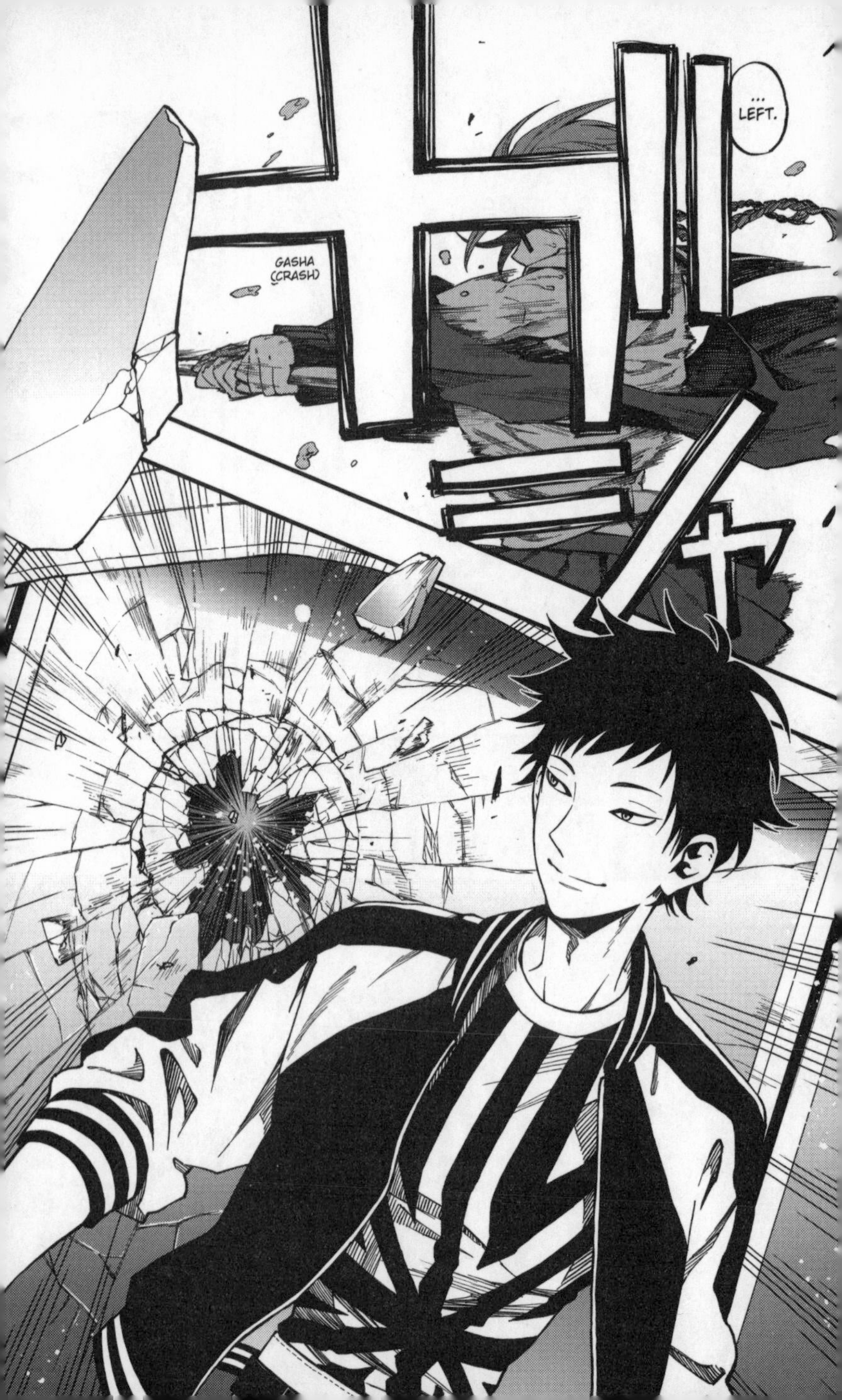

... LEFT.
GASHA (CRASH)

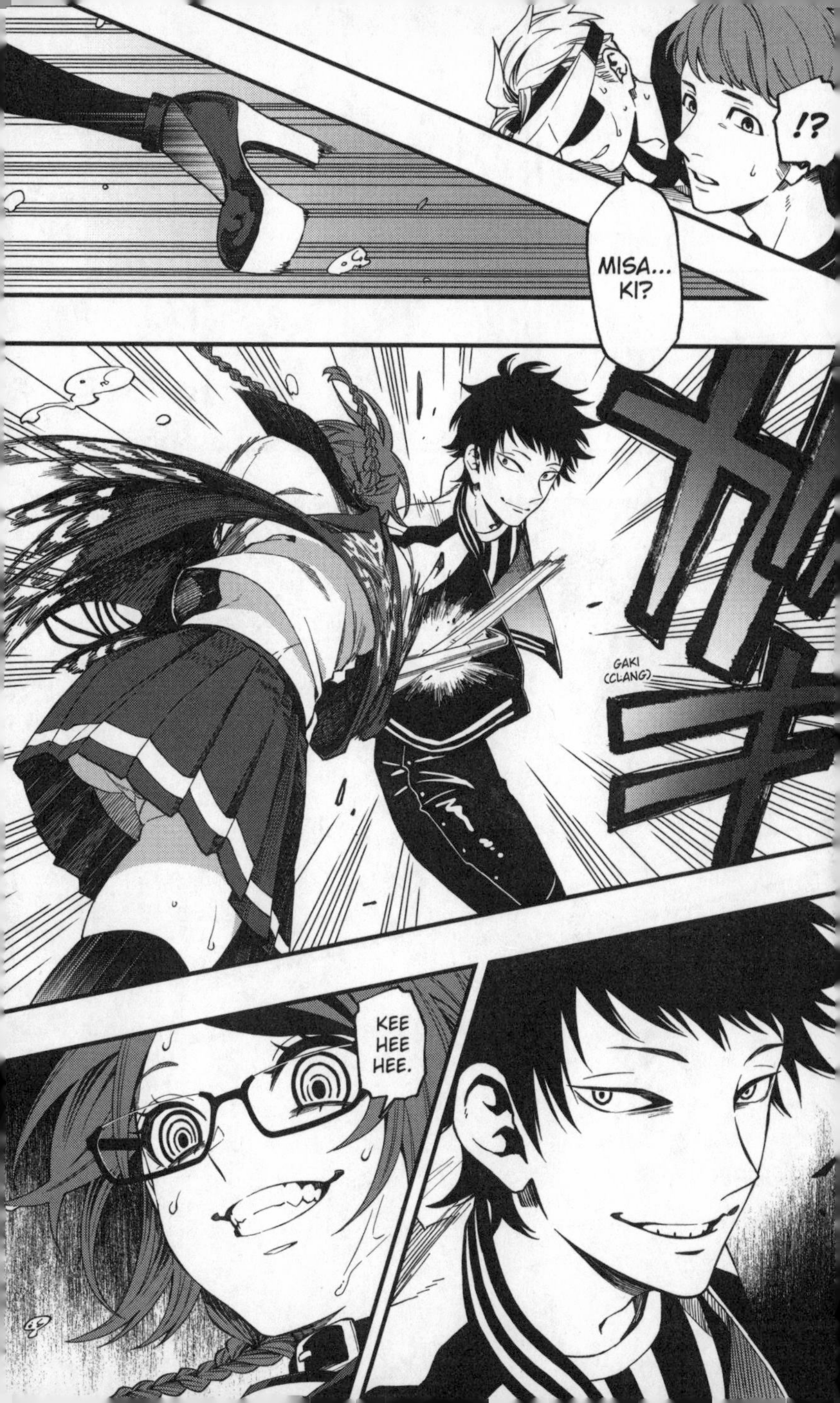
!?
MISA... KI?
GAKI (CLANG)
KEE HEE HEE.

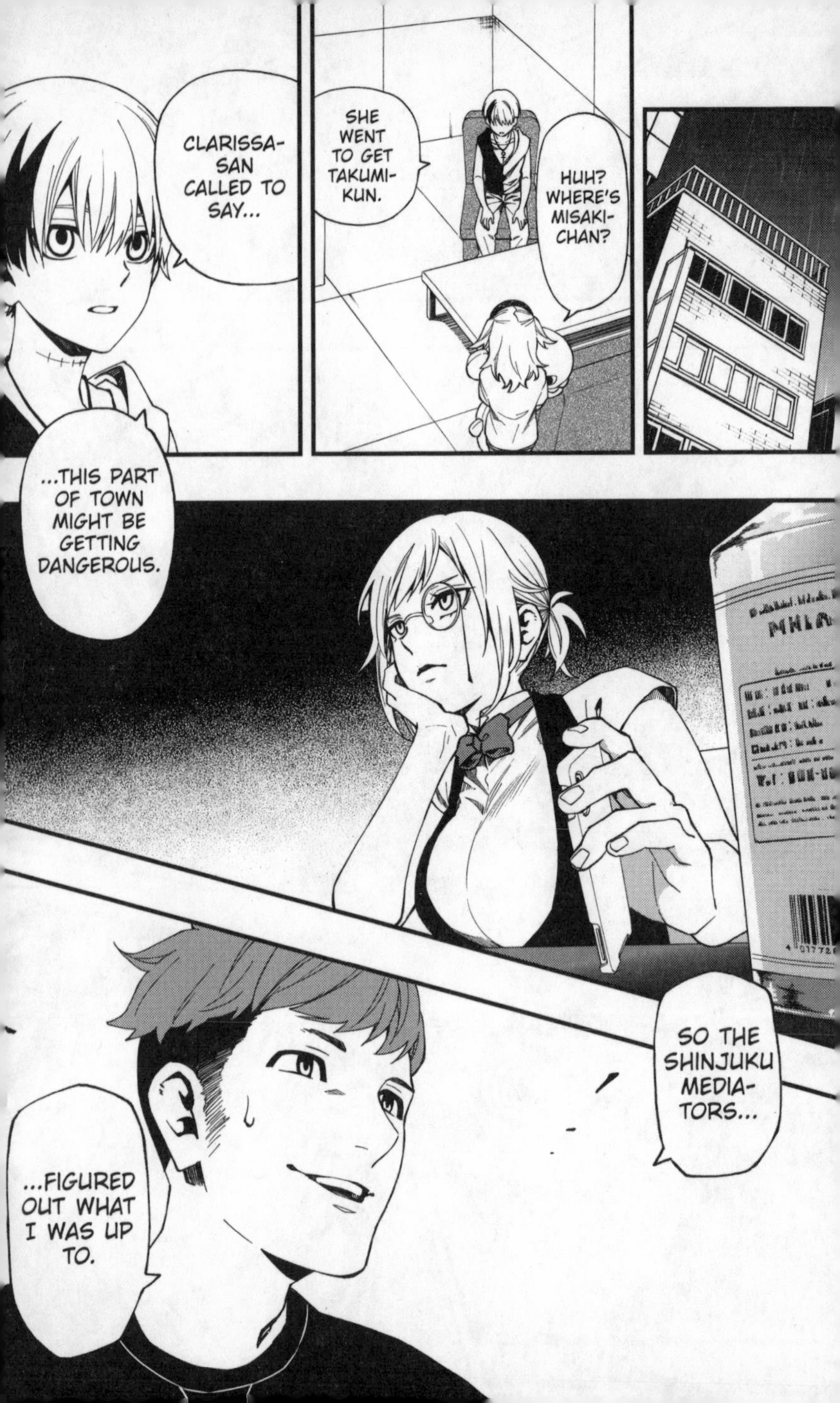
HUH? WHERE'S MISAKI-CHAN?
SHE WENT TO GET TAKUMI-KUN.
CLARISSA-SAN CALLED TO SAY...
...THIS PART OF TOWN MIGHT BE GETTING DANGEROUS.
SO THE SHINJUKU MEDIA-TORS...
...FIGURED OUT WHAT I WAS UP TO.

GA
(CLANG)

BIRI
BIRI
(STRAIN)

ZUZU
(SKID)

GO
(WHOOSH)

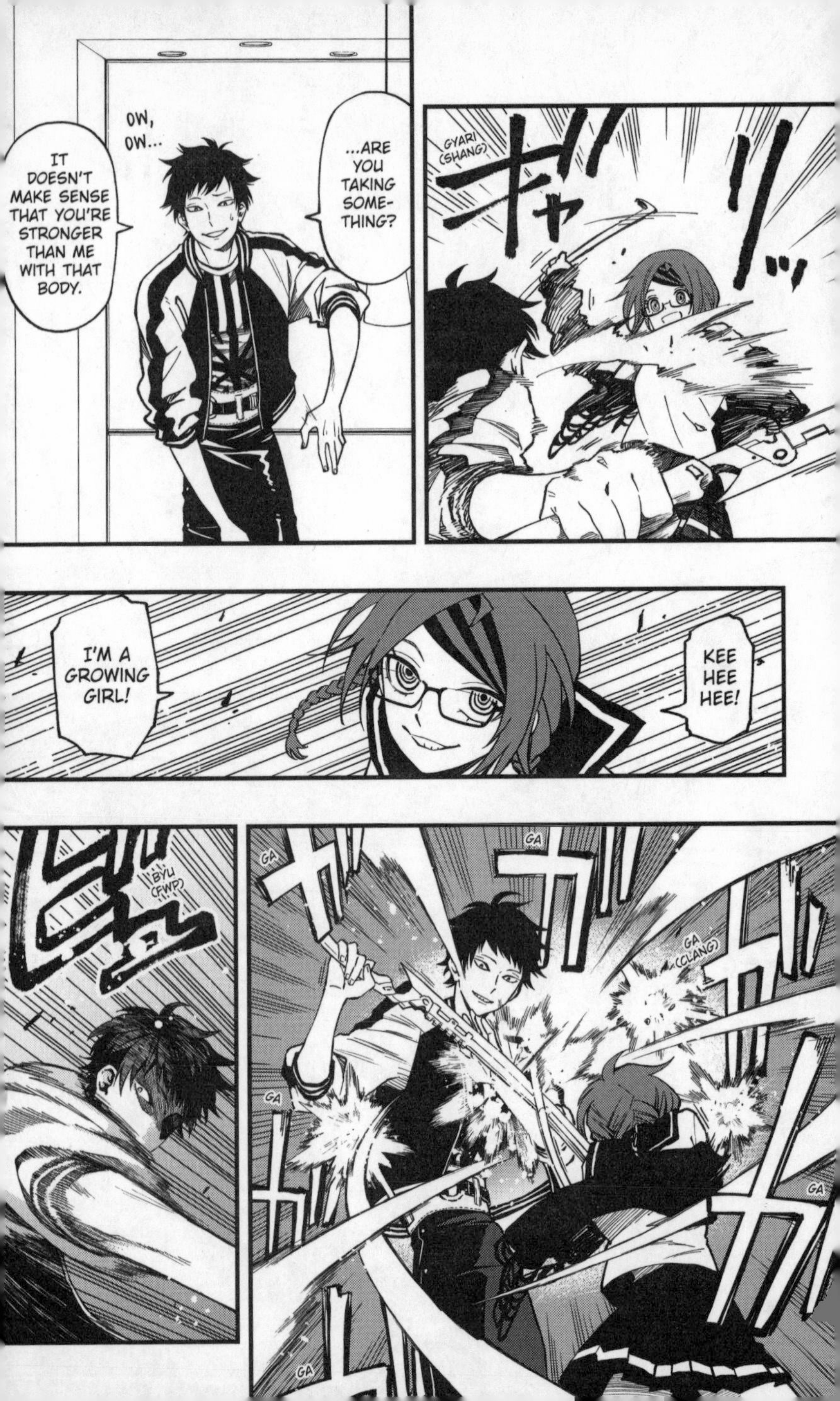
GYARI (SHANG)
...ARE YOU TAKING SOME-THING?
OW, OW...
IT DOESN'T MAKE SENSE THAT YOU'RE STRONGER THAN ME WITH THAT BODY.
KEE HEE HEE!
I'M A GROWING GIRL!
GA
GA
GA (CLANG)
GA
GA
GA
BYU (FWP)

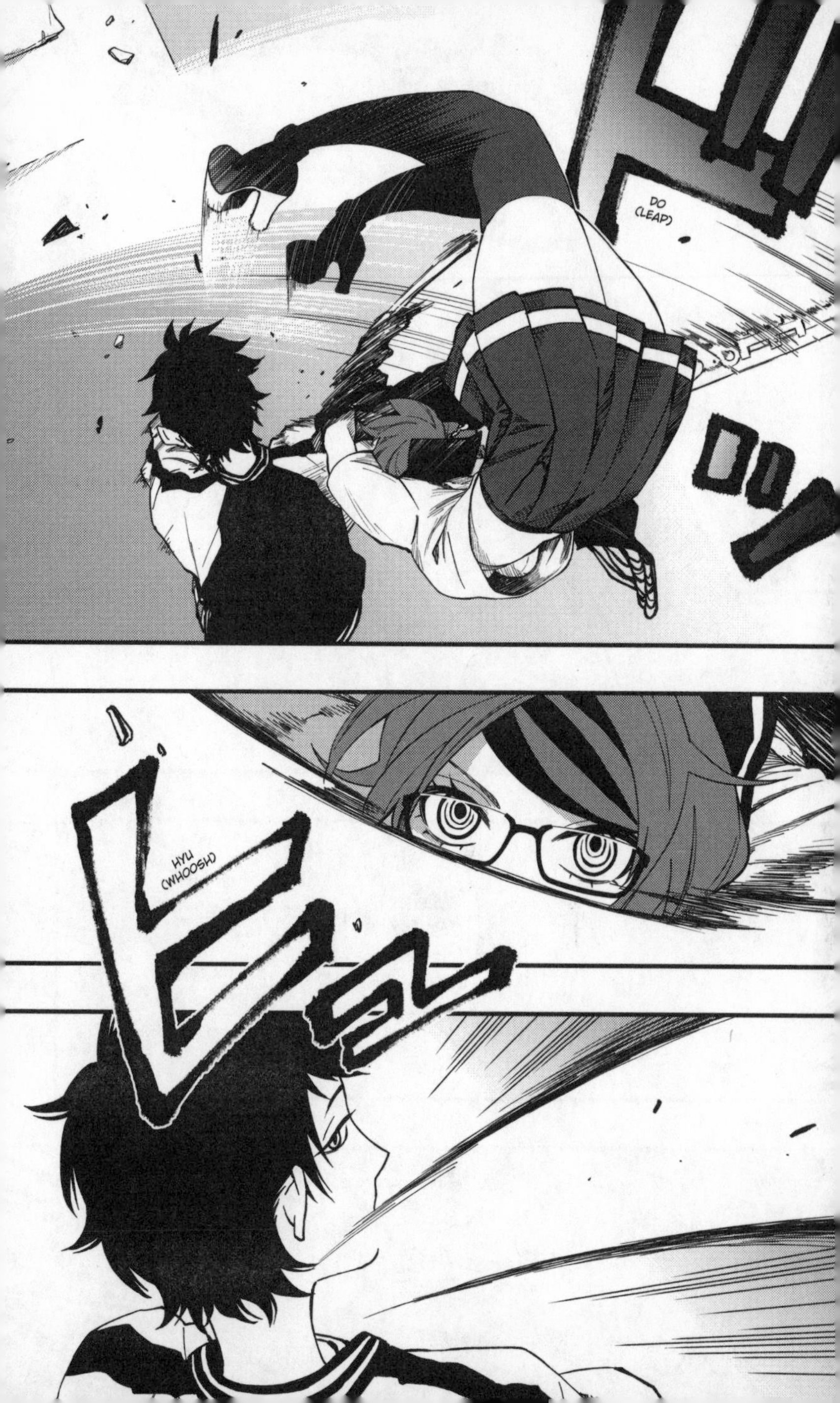
DO
(LEAP)
HYU
(WHOOSH)

GUNYA
(BEND)

MISSED
ME BY A
HAIR.

GASHA
(SHANG)

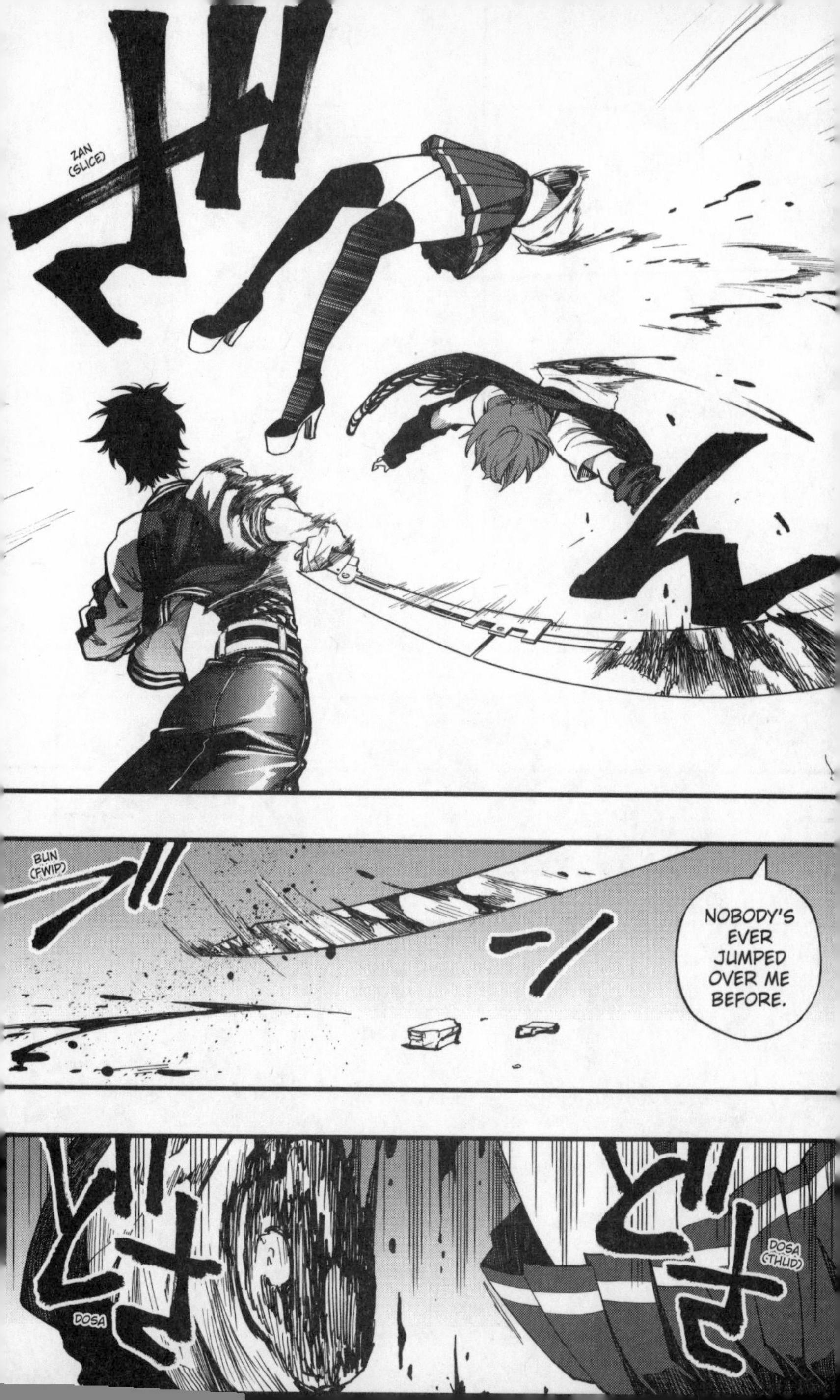
ZAN (SLICE)
BUN (FWIP)
NOBODY'S EVER JUMPED OVER ME BEFORE.
DOSA (THUD)
DOSA

MISA-KI...

HEY, MISA—

NO JOKE.

TSU (DRIBBLE)

...THAT WAS REALLY CLOSE.

HUH ...?

GURA (DIZZY)

NOW WAR IS DEFINITELY GOING TO BREAK OUT BETWEEN SHIBUYA AND SHINJUKU...

OH DEAR.

DOSA (THUD)

I'D RATHER NOT.

VUUUU (VRRR)

VUUUU

GOOD. IF I GET TO FIGHT WITH MORE KIDS LIKE THIS, I'LL GLADLY WELCOME IT, YOU KNOW?

I'LL GIVE YOU MY REPORT LATER.

THERE WAS A SLIGHT HICCUP.

...I'M SORRY.

...HEY.

...THERE CAN BE NO FAILURE.

UNDER THE PROTECTION OF SABARA-MOND...

I JUST HOPE...

HAAH...

...TAKUMI-KUN IS COOPERATIVE.

JIIIII
(ZIIIIP)

PATAN
(SHUT)
パタン

WHAT I CAN DO IS LIMITED.

YES.

ARE YOU SURE IT WAS OKAY TO USE THE GEMS FOR *THAT*?

HEY.

...HAVE MISAKI-CHAN EVOLVE INTO A NEW SPECIES, I THINK.

AND THAT'S...

IN FACT, I KNOW WHAT THE FIRST THING I'M GOING TO DO IS NOW THAT I HAVE THESE STONES IN HAND.

ZARA (FRSHH)

NOT ONLY WILL IT WIDEN MY HANDS OF PROTECTION...

BASA (FLAP)

...BUT I WANT TO INCREASE THE NUMBER OF ALLIES WHO CAN HELP ME PROTECT EVERYONE.

BOKO (BURBL)

EE!

EE!

BOKO

...IS NO LONGER A ZOMBIE.

NOW MISAKI-CHAN...

BASA
(FLAP)

BASA

SHE'S A VAMPIRE LARVA.

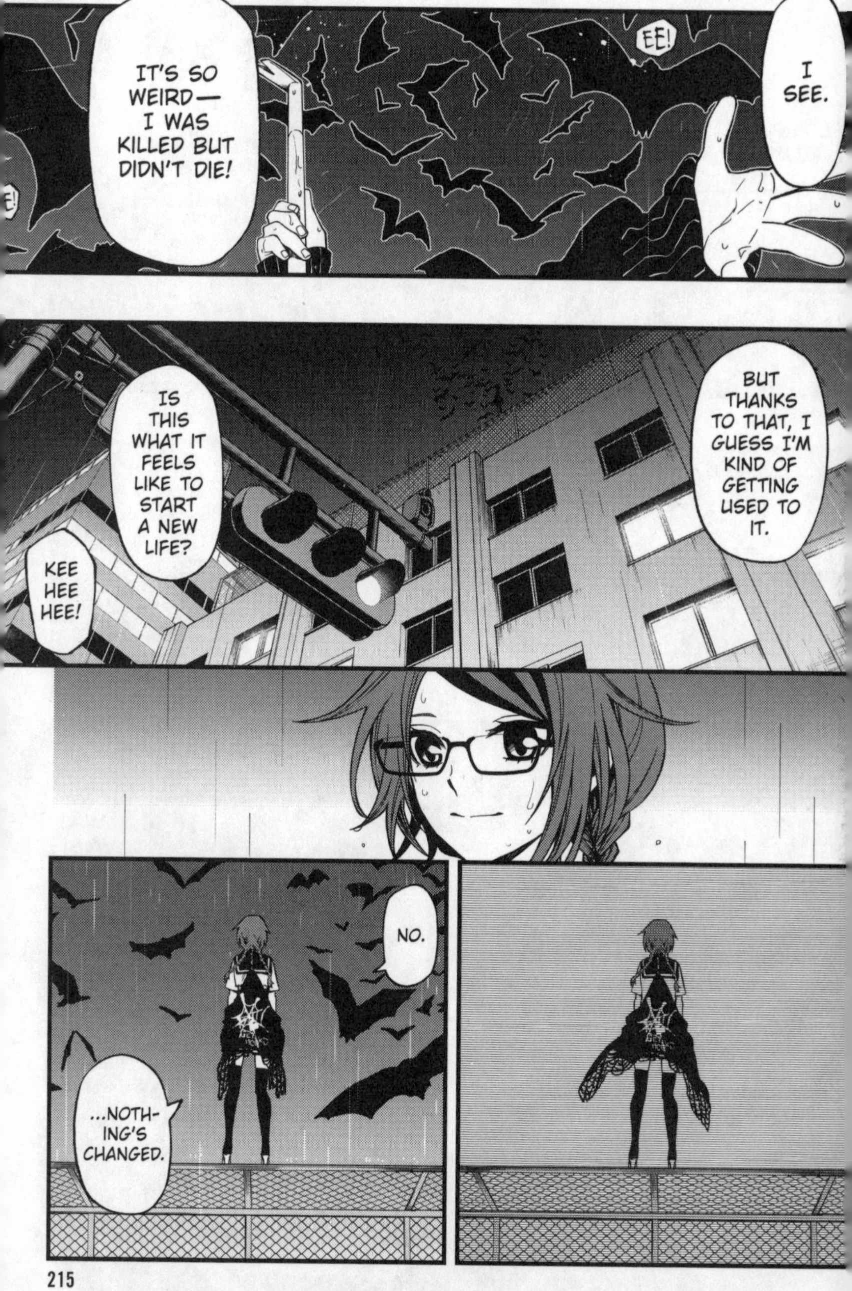
I SEE.
EE!
IT'S SO WEIRD—I WAS KILLED BUT DIDN'T DIE!
BUT THANKS TO THAT, I GUESS I'M KIND OF GETTING USED TO IT.
IS THIS WHAT IT FEELS LIKE TO START A NEW LIFE?
KEE HEE HEE!
NO.
...NOTHING'S CHANGED.

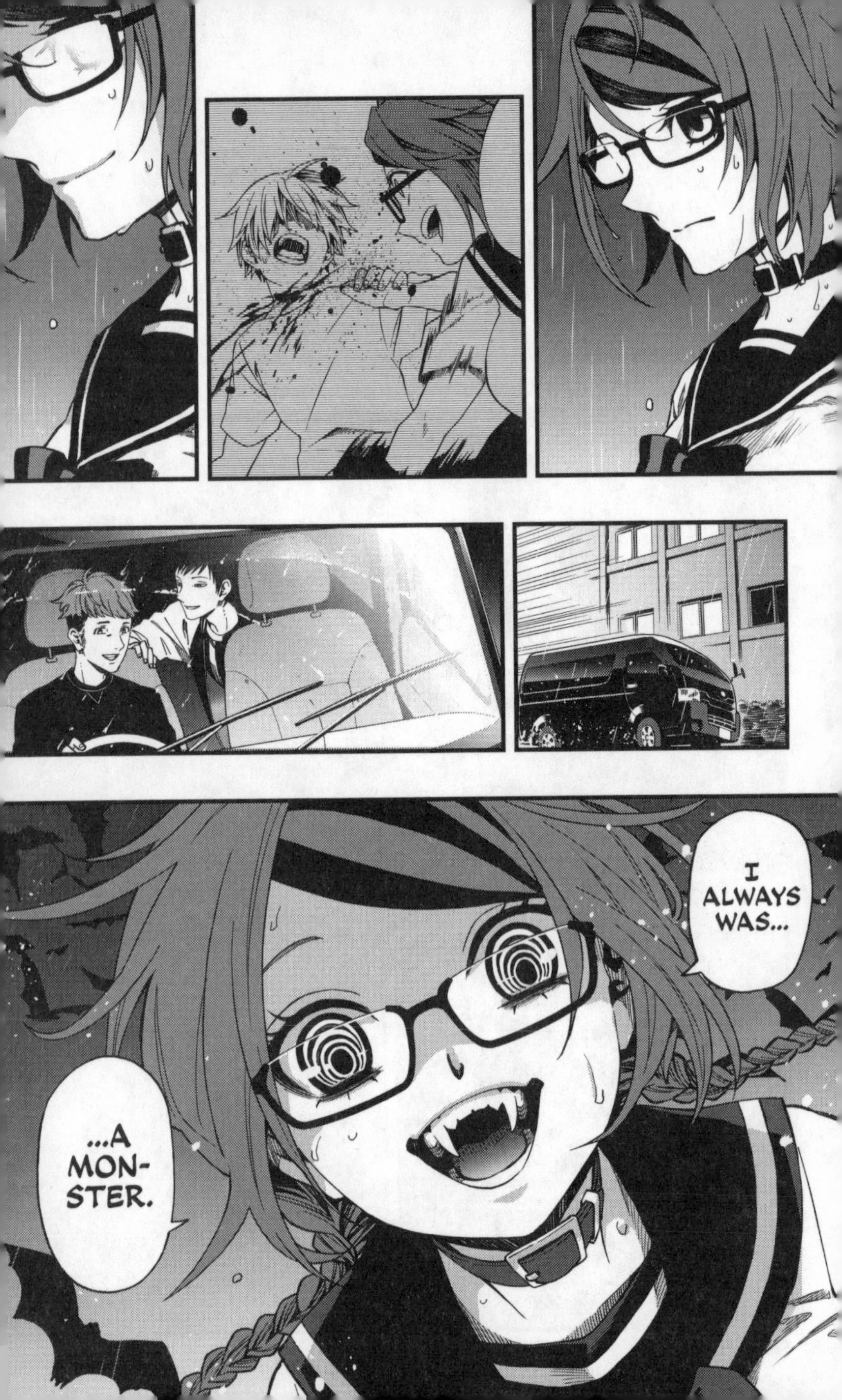
I ALWAYS WAS...
...A MON-STER.

DEAD MOUNT DEATH PLAY 5 END

MAKES SENSE, SINCE THIS ISN'T A RESIDENTIAL BUILDING.

...THE KITCHEN REALLY IS SMALL...

I'D GUESSED AS MUCH, BUT...

I'LL STICK THE LARGE STORAGE FRIDGE IN MY ROOM...

I'LL LEAVE THE SMALL FRIDGE HERE, SECURE SOME SPACE ABOVE IT TO STORE THE COOKWARE, AND THEN THE SPICES WILL GO......

IT'S FOR THE MISTRESS, SO I HAVE TO MAKE SURE HER MEALS ARE NUTRITIOUS!

LA-DI-DAAAAA...

IS POLKA MAKING SURE TO COOK HIS OWN MEALS......?

I'M OFF!

...THOSE TWO LEAVE FOR THEIR OWN HOMES AT NIGHT......

COME TO THINK OF IT...

I JUST GO TO THE CONVENIENCE STORE...

...AND SUCH.

OH!

UH...

IF YOU GET MALNOURISHED, AS THE NEAREST EMPLOYEE OF THE FAMILY, I'LL BE HELD RESPONSIBLE.

THIS ISN'T A MATTER OF MONEY.

I-IT'S OKAY, XIAOYU-KUN!

ZUI (SHOVE)

(RICE)

I CAN AFFORD MY MEALS.

WELL, THEN AT LEAST LET ME COVER THE GROCERY BILL......

SPECIAL THANKS!

WRITER:
RYOHGO NARITA

EDITOR:
KAZUHIDE SHIMIZU

TRANSLATION HELP:
JUYOUN LEE (YEN PRESS)

MAGIC RESEARCH:
KIYOMUNE MIWA (TEAM BARREL ROLL)

STAFF:
YOSHICHIKA EGUCHI
NORA
OTO
NANAMI HASAMA

Super-Fun Illustrated Guide to
DEAD MOUNT DEATH PLAY

THE SHARKBORG FROM HELL:
~ THE SHARK SIX ~
SPECIAL CONVENIENCE-STORE-RELEASE
SHARK PARFAIT

SIX VARIETIES
THAT DIDN'T
MAKE THE CUT.

A parfait designed to capture the moment Sharkborg surfaces in the ocean. The original plan was to make as many varieties as there are sharks in the series, but due to budget constraints, that idea was abandoned.

TRANSLATION NOTES

COMMON HONORIFICS

no honorific: Indicates familiarity or closeness; if used without permission or reason, addressing someone in this manner would constitute an insult.

-san: The Japanese equivalent of Mr./Mrs./Miss. If a situation calls for politeness, this is the fail-safe honorific.

-sama: Conveys great respect; may also indicate the social status of the speaker is lower than that of the addressee.

-kun: Used most often when referring to boys, this indicates affection or familiarity. Occasionally used by older men among their peers, but it may also be used by anyone referring to a person of lower standing.

-chan: An affectionate honorific indicating familiarity used mostly in reference to girls; also used in reference to cute persons or animals of either gender.

-senpai: A suffix used to address upperclassmen or more experienced coworkers.

-sensei: A respectful term for teachers, artists, or high-level professionals.

Page 90
Agakura is over two meters tall, or over six feet, five inches tall.

Page 95
The Yamanote Line is one of Tokyo's busiest railway lines. It runs through most of the major stations and urban centers in the area, including Shinjuku, Shibuya, Ikebukuro.

NEXT VOLUME PREVIEW

OTHER-WISE...I... WOULDN'T GET ANY-WHERE...

I'M STUB-BORN TOO...

I WISH YOU'D HELD ON TO THAT STUBBORNNESS BACK WHEN ARASE WAS THREATENING YOU.

"MY FRIENDS' LIVES ARE MUCH MORE VALUABLE THAN ANY SECRET OF MINE."

Feelings eddy in the twilight.

DEAD MOUNT DEATH PLAY

...I HAVE A LACKEY WHO'LL KEEP ME IN LINE EVEN IF HE HAS TO PUNCH ME TO DO IT.

Misaki, now brimming with freakish new powers, goes to rescue the kidnapped Takumi—but when she races to "Shinjuku," she finds an even more unfortunate fate awaiting her. It's a mad performance when two "nonhumans" clash. This is the true value of this group performance of "reincarnation." The "two worlds" mingling swallow up incidents and feelings from the past and tie it all together.

...I CAN GET AROUND IN THIS BODY LIKE IT'S SECOND NATURE!

EVEN THOUGH THIS IS ALL NEW TO ME...

I'M NOT A HEILE ANYMORE

TO BE CONTINUED.........

DEAD MOUNT DEATH PLAY

STORY: Ryohgo Narita ART: Shinta Fujimoto

Translation: Christine Dashiell ✳ Lettering: Abigail Blackman

DEAD MOUNT DEATH PLAY Volume 5 ©2020 Ryohgo Narita, Shinta Fujimoto/SQUARE ENIK CO., LTD. First published in Japan in 2020 by SQUARE ENIK CO., LTD. English translation rights arranged with SQUARE ENIK CO., LTD. and Yen Press, LLC through Tuttle-Mori Agency, Inc., Tokyo.

English translation ©2021 by SQUARE ENIX CO., LTD.

Yen Press
150 West 30th Street, 19th Floor
New York, NY 10001

Visit us at yenpress.com
facebook.com/yenpress
twitter.com/yenpress
yenpress.tumblr.com
instagram.com/yenpress

First Yen Press eBook Edition: May 2021
The chapters in this volume were originally published as ebooks by Yen Press.

Yen Press is an imprint of Yen Press, LLC.
The Yen Press name and logo are trademarks of Yen Press, LLC.

The publisher is not responsible for websites (or their content) that are not owned by the publisher.

Library of Congress Control Number: 2018953479

ISBNs: 978-1-9753-2444-5 (paperback)
       978-1-9753-2445-2 (ebook)

10 9 8 7 6 5 4 3 2 1

WOR

Printed in the United States of America

Turn to the back of the book to read an exclusive
bonus short story by Ryohgo Narita!

DEAD MOUNT DEATH PLAY
Episode ⑤: The Way of the Jesting Dragons

Now read the latest chapters of BLACK BUTLER digitally at the same time as Japan and support the creator!

The Phantomhive family has a butler who's almost too good to be true...

...or maybe he's just too good to be human.

Black Butler

YANA TOBOSO

VOLUMES 1-29 IN STORES NOW!

Yen Press
www.yenpress.com

BLACK BUTLER © Yana Toboso / SQUARE ENIX
Yen Press is an imprint of Yen Press, LLC.

OLDER TEEN
OT

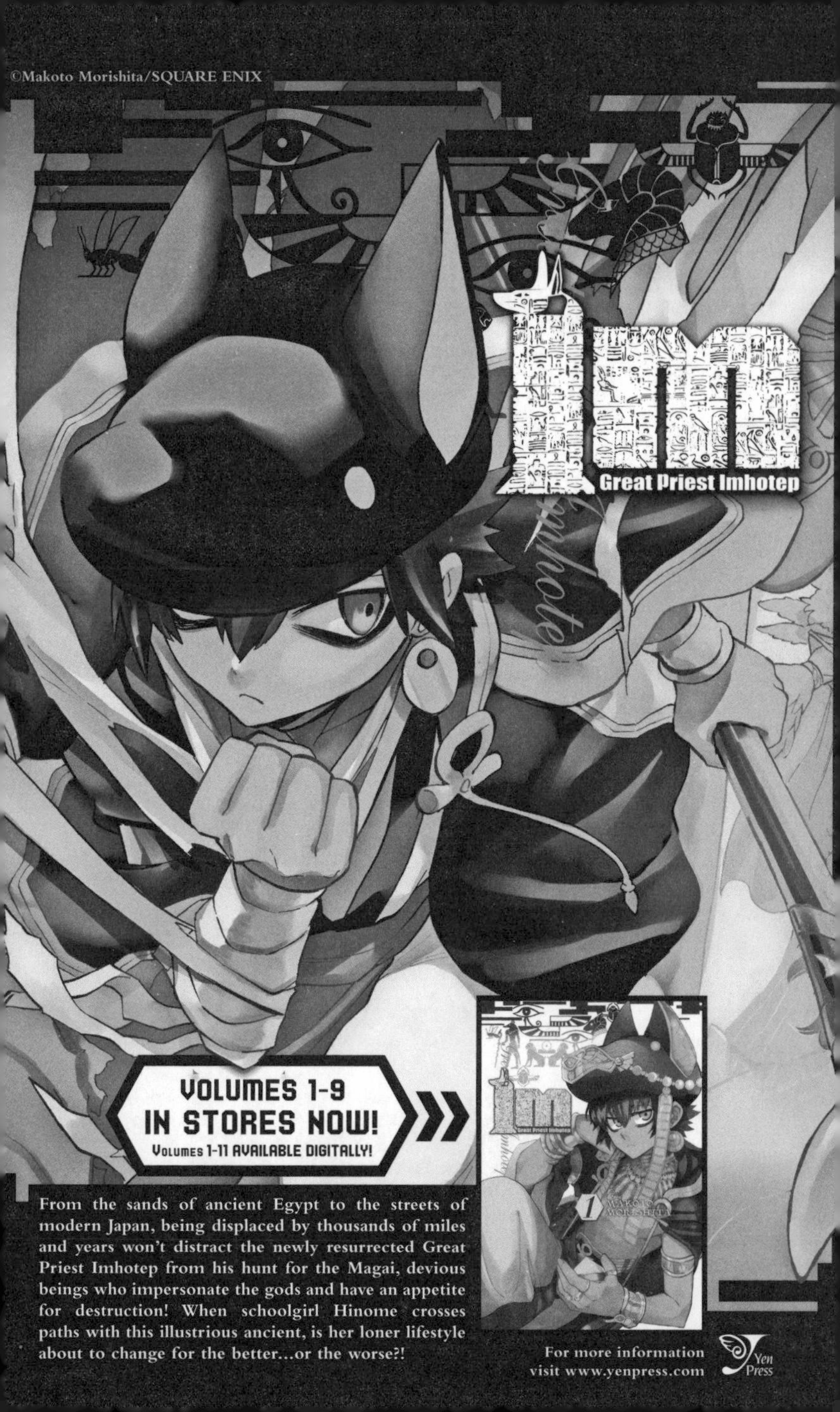
©Makoto Morishita/SQUARE ENIX
Im
Great Priest Imhotep
VOLUMES 1-9
IN STORES NOW!
VOLUMES 1-11 AVAILABLE DIGITALLY!
Im
Great Priest Imhotep
1
MAKOTO MORISHITA
From the sands of ancient Egypt to the streets of modern Japan, being displaced by thousands of miles and years won't distract the newly resurrected Great Priest Imhotep from his hunt for the Magai, devious beings who impersonate the gods and have an appetite for destruction! When schoolgirl Hinome crosses paths with this illustrious ancient, is her loner lifestyle about to change for the better...or the worse?!
For more information
visit www.yenpress.com
Yen Press

Toilet-bound Hanako-Kun

At Kamome Academy, rumors abound about the school's Seven Mysteries, one of which is Hanako-san. Said to occupy the third stall of the third floor girls' bathroom in the old school building, Hanako-san grants any wish when summoned. Nene Yashiro, an occult-loving high school girl who dreams of romance, ventures into this haunted bathroom...but the Hanako-san she meets there is nothing like she imagined! Kamome Academy's

HE DOES NOT LET ANYONE ROLL THE DICE.

A young Priestess joins her first adventuring party, but blind to the dangers, they almost immediately find themselves in trouble. It's Goblin Slayer who comes to their rescue—a man who has dedicated his life to the extermination of all goblins by any means necessary. A dangerous, dirty, and thankless job, but he does it better than anyone. And when rumors of his feats begin to circulate, there's no telling who might come calling next...

Light Novel V. 1-11 Available Now!

Check out the simul-pub manga chapters every month!

Yen Press · YEN ON

www.yenpress.com

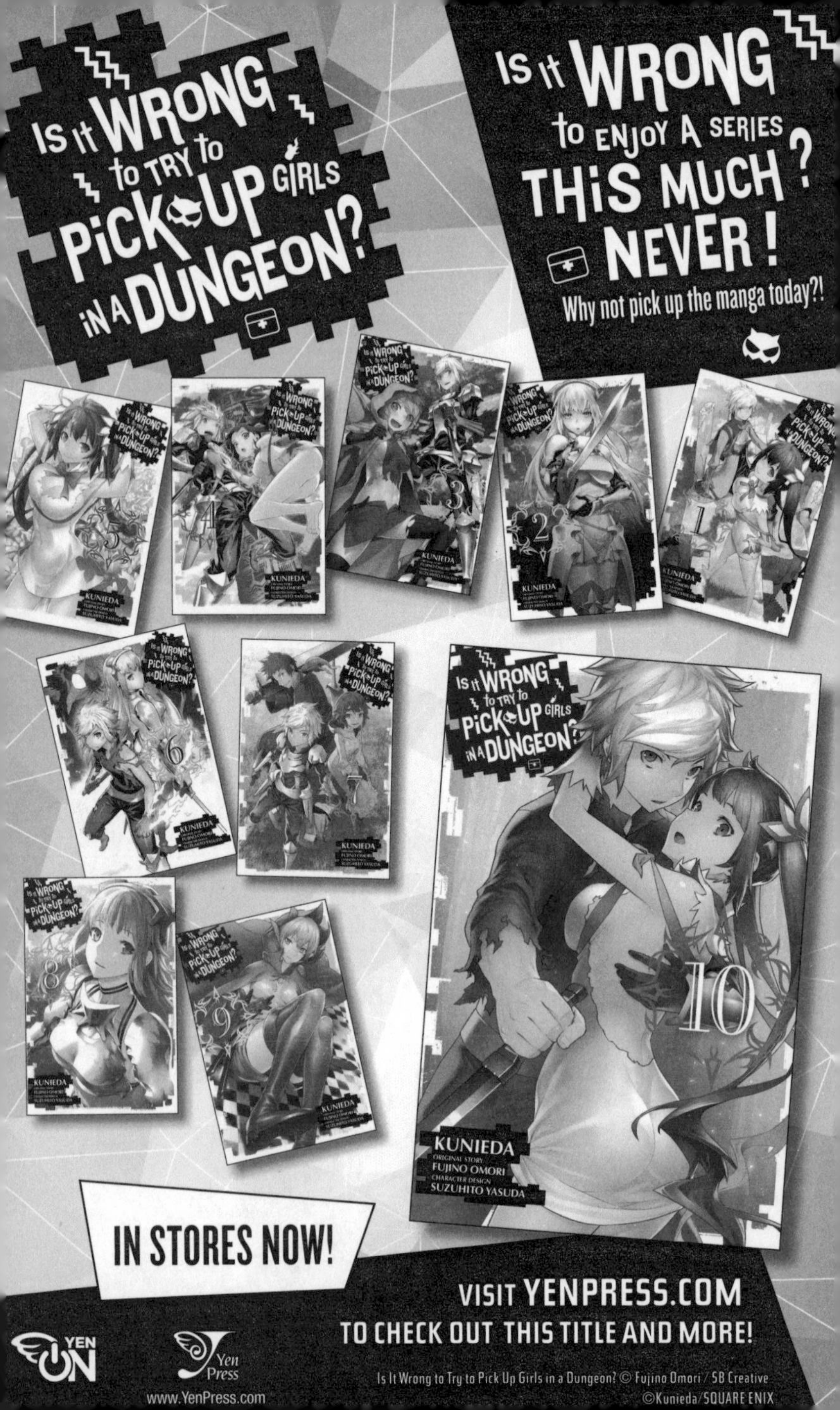

IS IT WRONG TO TRY TO PICK UP GIRLS IN A DUNGEON?
IS IT WRONG TO ENJOY A SERIES THIS MUCH? NEVER!
Why not pick up the manga today?!
IS IT WRONG TO TRY TO PICK UP GIRLS IN A DUNGEON?
10
KUNIEDA
ORIGINAL STORY
FUJINO OMORI
CHARACTER DESIGN
SUZUHITO YASUDA
IN STORES NOW!
VISIT YENPRESS.COM
TO CHECK OUT THIS TITLE AND MORE!
YEN ON
Yen Press
www.YenPress.com
Is It Wrong to Try to Pick Up Girls in a Dungeon? © Fujino Omori / SB Creative
©Kunieda/SQUARE ENIX

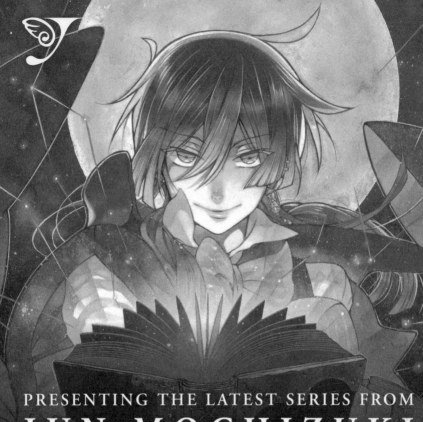

PRESENTING THE LATEST SERIES FROM
JUN MOCHIZUKI

THE CASE STUDY OF VANITAS

READ THE CHAPTERS AT THE SAME TIME AS JAPAN!

AVAILABLE NOW WORLDWIDE WHEREVER E-BOOKS ARE SOLD!

It was a lineup of technological progression, so to speak.

In addition, a stockpile of firearms and ammunition, similar to what had been used during the First World War, lay ready.

However, each item had been altered from its original state, improved upon in the last hundred years using the developments of this world to alter their designs and capabilities.

"It wasn't easy re-creating the 'Haber-Bosch process' or whatever it's called, but......the difficulty was well worth the overwhelming profits it's yielded. Yes. Ah yes. Though I have mass-produced this much weaponry, if the civilization it came from still hasn't crumbled, then they have probably given rise to even greater technology over the past hundred years."

As though speaking her words to a distant land, the smallest hint of true feeling crept into her voice as the Saint of the Geldwood Church, Elsia Sabaramond, turned up the corners of her mouth in pleasure.

"Soon I might like to open a new 'door'......dear brother Arius."

On the surface, rather than a single founder or pope, a representative system of nineteen head priests allegedly held the religion together. In reality, the person who sat in that twentieth seat—that is, the saint—was the central figure who made everything and anything happen.

At present, that saint was currently three floors below the meeting room where the round table stood.

"So Domdaal's life has been snuffed out...... Let me see, then either Recuria managed to get a blow in, or somebody else interfered and finished him off...... Considering the energy signature of my spy team has vanished as well, it's most likely the latter."

The murmured words came from a woman who could be no older than twenty, who swept her beautiful silver hair to the side with a slight smile.

Though she was clad in the standard white Geldwood Church ceremonial raiments, the woman looked more bewitchingly mysterious rather than neat and tidy, and as she gazed into the sparkle of the magical pan filled with water before her, she continued speaking to herself.

"It couldn't be Calamity Crusher, could it......? Impossible. It must either be a sect of alchemy scholars or Wandering Balcony. Or perhaps some dragon stuck its snout where it doesn't belong."

Her smile held no emotion whatsoever and was merely plastered on to hide her true feelings. But even so, it was a smile of such beauty that it was still enough to deceive others.

Not that she would ever show that face to anyone. She merely continued to murmur as she looked up at the empty space above her in the dark room.

"It seems we still have many enemies," she whispered, slowly turning around to look at something behind her. "We mustn't waste any time...... raising the standard of our equipment."

There was a line of objects occupying the space behind her.

Each of them would have been incomprehensible to the people of this world if they were to lay eyes on them.

But...the inhabitants of some other world might get a wholly different, clearer impression.

A projector, a Tesla coil, models of aircraft and carrier jets, radio-communication equipment, and engines of every shape and size.

"If it means having to get involved with the Geldwood gang again, I'd rather travel through the hole that once opened here long ago and head to Terra Mater or some other such place...... Though, I hear that the magic essence is weak there, so...... Oh well, it might not be too late to ask Ordom for help...... Kuh-kuh."

Shagrua cocked his head at the peculiar mutterings Pirawizzo had slipped into, but a stronger question for the trio rose up in his mind.

"Wait...... Why are you so wary of the Geldwood Church?"

It was Izliz who wasted no time answering his inquiry.

"As I said before, I don't hate Geldwood enough that I want to massacre them all. The ones I loathe are the guys at the top. I never want to see the faces of fifteen of their nineteen head priests."

"In particular, the twentieth head priest of the nineteen...... I've never liked the saint of that religion."

■■■

Central Bol Continent
Sacred Mount Boldorazo

Far to the north of the Byandy Peninsula was the continent's tallest mountain chain, which towered over the Kingdom of Nyanild, the Principality of Djadjamnyl, and two other small countries.

At the heart of the tallest of those tall mountains, space for a single city had been painstakingly dug out.

The imposing building standing at its center was not the royal palace, but a massive "church."

It belonged to the Church of Geldwood, designated as the official religion of a number of countries, including the Kingdom of Nyanild.

The cathedral built into that mountain and deemed a holy site was much larger than the one in the Kingdom of Nyanild, and its form seemed to embody the control and power the Church held over this continent.

Below the Church was a space where the nineteen head priests who led the faithful would gather, but twenty seats were arranged at the round table that stood in the center.

Shagrua hesitated only a moment before a strong conviction overtook him and prompted him to start talking.

He told them of his battle against the Corpse God...and the truth he had discovered afterward.

Then he told them how he had completely cut ties with the Church—and his true goal for coming to this peninsula.

"I swear, that foolish pupil of mine...... I see he still hasn't changed his tendency to take on all his problems alone. What were those spirits who contracted themselves to him thinking, I wonder."

After she had heard his entire story, Izliz shrugged and went on, "I see...... So you came to see to the restoration of this peninsula, did you? That's quite a mission."

"Yes...... But if any of you have a reason why that shouldn't happen, then I would like to hear it."

In response to Shagrua's doubts, the human-child Pirawizzo snickered.

"Kuh-kuh...... This place is a paradise out of the reach of anybody in the Geldwood order. If it was developed, it would have to be done carefully, or neighboring countries would probably get involved. Which means those with Geldwood really would get their hands on it."

"Those with Geldwood......?"

Picking up where Pirawizzo had left off, Romelka spoke up, causing a stir in the surrounding forest.

"This peninsula itself is a relic of our empire—and our heritage as well. If it was to fall into the hands of the people of Geldwood, there could be a repeat of the Day of Destruction—or perhaps an event of even greater devastation. If that happened, it wouldn't be just our problem, but the whole continent itself would be in danger...... So, uh, we've been protecting the legacy of the empire to keep it from falling into anyone's hands, least of all the Geldwood Church's!"

"And you're helping in this effort as well, Pirawizzo?"

"I just happen to like this region for how thick with magical essence it is, so that is why I've hung around. Granted, thanks to that, I often get mixed up in annoying problems."

As though acknowledging something unspoken among themself and Izliz and Romelka, Pirawizzo let out a sigh, keeping their eyes glued to the two women.

"No...... I'm just shocked to learn you're such a talker."

Izliz shrugged as though in agreement.

"It's amazing how Pirawizzo and Romelka can go on and on when they're fired up, isn't it? If you let them be, they'd go for three days and nights straight without stopping. When you've lived as long as we have, you either go quiet or become a chatterbox—there is no in-between."

"Hmph. That's only because it's tiring to speak human tongue while in my dragon form. If I'm going to use human language, I'll take a human form, just as when speaking cat language I take cat form, and when speaking with Elementals, it's best to take the form of an Elemental."

"I see......" Shagrua wasn't agreeing with what had just been said about language but was nodding his understanding of why Pirawizzo had killed the kings, and he dipped his head low.

"I'm......sorry that happened to you."

"What?"

Pirawizzo made an expression of confusion, as if a surprised Shagrua was capable of lowering his head to anyone. They cocked their head, waiting for Shagrua to go on.

"I had always simply taken at face value the stories that you suddenly invaded the country and killed the former king unprovoked. Of course, had I asked you, I probably wouldn't have believed you so easily, but even so, I should have at least asked you your reasons before I fought you."

"Hold it, hold it, Calamity Crusher. Don't you think suddenly swallowing my side of the story now is even more unreasonable?"

"Well...... That might be so, but......compared to what I heard from the leaders of the Geldwood Church, listening to your side of the story has more value."

"......Is that why you're here? Calamity Crusher, have you cut ties with the Church?"

Pirawizzo's face had taken on a gentle look, and at their question, Izliz nodded in agreement.

"That's right. And that reminds me, I haven't asked you the details surrounding your visit here. It's the least you could do after we patched you up. Would you mind telling me?"

"......All right."

What stood before them now was a child of indeterminate gender.

But judging by the style of their speech, they were clearly Pirawizzo, and Shagrua concluded the dragon had used Humanize, a magic spell employed by dragons that he had heard tales of.

As Shagrua looked on with wide eyes, Pirawizzo spoke to him in a high voice befitting his tiny stature.

"Hmph. What is it now, Calamity Crusher?! Are you getting all caught up in the silly issue of whether I'm a boy or a girl? Do you really think dragons even have the kind of gender assignments that apply to humans and lizards? Dragons are a kind that individually evolve to the extreme. Unlike humans, who only have a handful of attributes for male, female, and a few others, you should remember that we have as many genders as there are dragons."

"I see and understand your point...... Thank you for explaining it to me."

"You're more cooperative than I thought, Calamity Crusher! Then you should listen, keeping that cooperative nature as your central pillar! I didn't eat those kings to fill an empty stomach. Each and every one of them wanted the blood of the Poisonous Dragon of Destruction so they could use it as an ultimate weapon against other countries. *They* tried to kill *me*, so I had no choice but to defend myself! The former king of Nyanild was hilarious, you know that? He said he wanted to form a pact between his country and dragons, so I strolled right in to start the talks when, wouldn't you know, he betrayed me immediately! Apparently, he thought that some magic barrier set up by the Church or something could curb my powers. He'd believed blindly that what had worked on Giralzigul and Zari would work on me, but his foolishness cost him his life. I put on a little show like I was suffering, writhing around and crying out "Gweeh!" and he had the gall to mock me and stomp on my head. But the way he lost his composure and begged for his life once he realized I actually could move was a bit entertaining, so I killed him without making him suffer too much!"

"......"

"Hmm? What's the matter, Calamity Crusher? Is my dainty human form confusing you? Or can you not believe how despicable your country's former king was?"

Shagrua had fallen silent, but he shook his head once and answered Pirawizzo, interrupting the dragon's fit of amused laughter.

"What's this? You two seem awfully chummy."

"This is what I'd call a touching reunion! Fated rivals who at one time tried to kill each other, now run into each other again under different circumstances at a different time and place. Why, it's a regular old romance. You could even call it destiny! Once, they wanted each other's lives, but now it's a picturesque fairy tale of love and camaraderie! I wonder if they even realize how essential they've become to each other's lives. I hope they figure it out soon—preferably right now! Please, please realize it; thank you!"

Ignoring the ripple from the forest as it grew excited with its own rampant delusions, Shagrua spoke to the dragon before him.

"What are you doing in this land? The country here has already fallen......"

"?"

"There is no king or emperor for you to feast upon."

"......What do you take me to be? Do you humans actually think I killed those rulers to satisfy an empty belly?"

At his words, Shagrua suddenly remembered.

He had left his country after realizing the "truths" he had been told all his life were false, and he was now working to overturn his own concept of what was "common sense." Given all that had happened, he reasoned he would probably have to start afresh when it came to everything he previously had taken for granted.

Even where it concerned a villainous dragon who had terrorized people.

"......Am I wrong? That's what I had been told where I come from......"

"Don't be ridiculous. I can only take so much slander."

Upon hearing that, Izliz let out a chuckle by his side and interjected.

"It's true. Ninety-nine percent of the empire's people believed that, Pirawizzo. From what the theatrical promoters and dragon scholars say, you relish the flesh of powerful men as a delicacy, and you use their high-born souls to prolong your own life span."

"......"

There was a moment of silence.

Whorls of wind in seven colors stirred up around Pirawizzo, and a second later, a miniature human silhouette came into view from within.

"Hold it right there, Wandering Balcony Izliz! I thought you knew! How could you have let rumors about me run wild like that?!"

■■■

The Byandy Peninsula
Ruins of the Empire

"Kuh-kah, kuh-kah-kah-kah-kah! What's the matter, Calamity Crusher? Your soul's gone stiff."

This dragon Shagrua had thought was long gone now glided down from the ceiling, roughly the size of a large ox. However, Shagrua's Evil Eye recognized the situation for what it really was.

It could see that condensed within the small dragon before him was a density of souls equal to dozens of mountain-size dragons.

Despite having a very miniature stature for a dragon, this monster of monsters, who could overwhelm the giant, castle-size Dragon Emperor Wriggler through physical strength alone, was acting nothing like a monster as it rationally conversed to Shagrua in a low voice.

"Compared to before, you're much more...human-seeming now."

"......Human-seeming?" Shagrua couldn't help repeating, never dropping his guard. And yet, he could neither agree to nor deny it.

The weapon in my hand......

When he looked, he found his suit of armor placed beside the bed where he'd been sleeping until just a moment before.

Without the Church's—Recuria and company's—help, and while still recovering from the injuries he'd sustained in his fight against Izliz, he couldn't imagine he'd stand a chance against the beast, no matter how hard he was to struggle.

On the other hand, this was not an opponent who he could simply retreat from.

Pirawizzo didn't seem interested in fighting at present, but Shagrua had heard that most dragons had fickle dispositions and wasn't prepared to let his guard down one iota. He was running through various scenarios in his mind to determine the best course of action, when...

By his side, the Necromancer Izliz and Wood Mage Romelka began to talk at once.

When it comes to taking down a dragon, one may rely on a potion wrought by a sorcerer, a tincture developed by science, an illness brought on by a microbe invisible to the naked eye, something that has always existed in the natural world, erosion caused by an incomprehensible ancient curse, the inescapable phenomenon of death itself, and so forth... But anything that might have felled Pirawizzo was immediately thwarted by that which flowed through his very veins: a "dragon poison" that would destroy all things besides himself. If ever he was attacked by sword, arrow, bombardment, or spell, the blood he spilled destroyed his attacker in turn and made the very land he stood on wither away.

He neutralized every effort to poison him and wreaked havoc on the world with his own blood.

This was what earned him the title of the Poisonous Dragon of Destruction.

Furthermore, Pirawizzo had opposed numerous kingdoms and empires in the past and slaughtered the kings and emperors who ruled them, so that he was feared in every region of the land as the Former King Killer and Late Emperor Killer.

At the end of the war, for the honor and dignity of the Geldwood Church, Shagrua had managed to successfully drive the dragon out of the territory of Nyanild, though he didn't have the nerve to call it any kind of victory.

It half-seemed as if he had been left unchallenged.

At the time of their last confrontation, he suspected Pirawizzo still had power to spare.

After unleashing his most powerful attack, Pirawizzo used his poison as a smoke screen and disappeared.

The leaders in the Church assumed he must have fled in fear for his life, but from where he had stood on the front lines, Shagrua hadn't sensed an ounce of fear or terror coming from Pirawizzo.

And Shagrua still sensed that from them.

Their last meeting had been years ago.

Far from Nyanild in the Byandy Empire, the Poisonous Dragon of Destruction Pirawizzo, who now rose up before him did not give off the faintest hint of being afraid or on his guard. In fact, he had the air of one meeting an old friend as he spoke to Shagrua with the utmost confidence.

Though they were in the minority, the extreme aggression of these dragons left huge, gaping scars of a degree that changed the very course of human history, and in many tales—or rather, the majority of religious texts—dragons collectively were regarded as "evil."

They say the Sand Destroyer Dragon, Giralzigul, dried up the longest river on the main continent in a mere day.

They say the Home-wrecker Dragon, Malfy, seduced the three kings and incited a war.

They say the Vapor Dragon, Goronzon, obscured the skies of a certain city with clouds over the course of ten years.

They say the Round Blade Dragon, Marm, demanded a living sacrifice of fifty blacksmiths every month.

They say the Burning Armor Dragon, Zari, reignited numerous inactive volcanoes, wiping out an entire country with the ensuing lava.

They say the Insect Master Dragon, Gremjarno, devastated twenty island nations with a swarm of insects that filled their sea.

They say the Bedroom Tower Dragon, Alaphon, relentlessly killed all the men of a certain country.

They say the Widower Dragon, Halyvon, completely wiped out all the women of a certain country.

They say the Hell Killer Dragon, Lala, ate two of his predecessors and didn't even care to guide the survivors of the two countries.

They say the Jester Dragon, Norda, is still writing boring comedy scripts and sends them to theater troupes on a daily basis to this day.

They say the Destructive Wyvern, Ordom, bent the laws of space and created a fissure that connects the reverse side of the skies to everlasting darkness.

They say, they say, they say...

Many dragons were notorious throughout the land, and Shagrua understood that the majority of them were not mere fairy tales but hard facts.

However, Shagrua had only directly encountered one dragon.

The beast had killed the former king of Nyanild, bringing the entire country close to ruin. Shagrua had spent three months locked in a life-and-death struggle with this envoy of destruction:

The Poisonous Dragon of Destruction Pirawizzo.

DEAD MOUNT DEATH PLAY

Episode ⑤: The Way of the Jesting Dragons

by Ryohgo Narita

Manga exclusive bonus short story

"We share this world with dragons."

Those were the cliché first words of many a fairy tale Shagrua had heard over the years.

Wyvern. Firedrake. Dragon.

In other words, dragons were real, living creatures of myth in Shagrua's world.

However...dragons were often treated like monsters or the messengers of wicked gods who threatened the world. Only a few rare exceptions—such as the Holy Dragon Nirai and the Mother Dragon Frenes Larx—were regarded as allies to mankind.

In the northern tip of the continent of Bol, where Shagrua was raised, there were many polytheistic countries that worshipped dragons as gods. Because these nations never established diplomatic relations with the Kingdom of Nyanild, however, he was unfamiliar with the details of their customs.

In reality, of the species referred to as "dragons," as many as half of them aggressively did harm to humans.

Even so, the majority only attacked as much as any other giant carnivore looking for food would. Only a miniscule handful of dragons who had lived long enough to develop intelligence harmed humans with purely malicious intent.